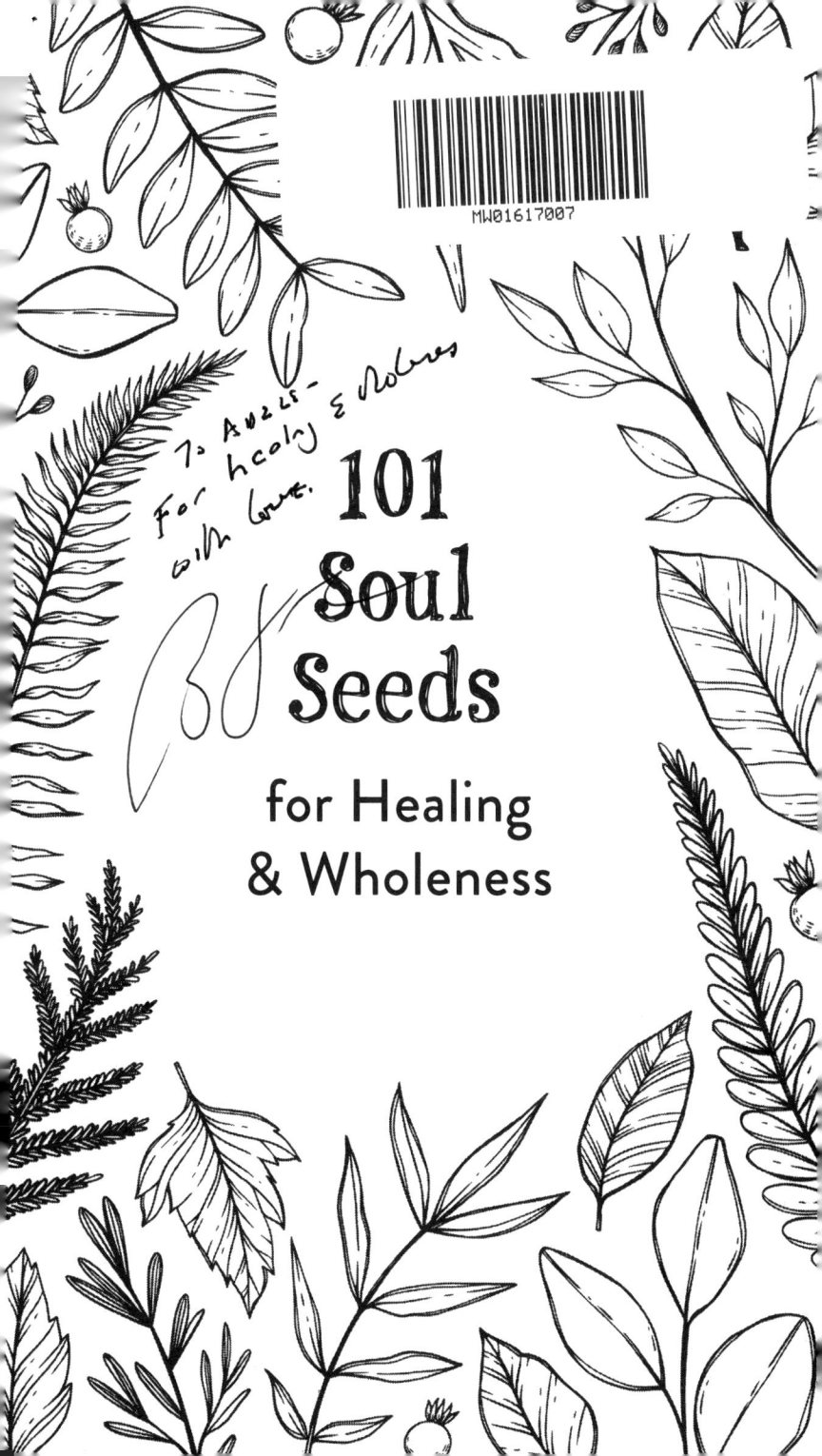

To Aurli—
For healing & wholeness
with love.

101
Soul
Seeds

for Healing
& Wholeness

ANAMCHARA BOOKS
Vestal, New York 13850
www.AnamcharaBooks.com

Paperback ISBN: 978-1-62524-832-9
Ebook ISBN: 978-1-62524-833-6

Cover design and interior layout by Micaela Grace.
Plant drawings by KateMyKate (Dreamstime.com).

101
Soul Seeds

for Healing
& Wholeness

BRUCE G. EPPERLY

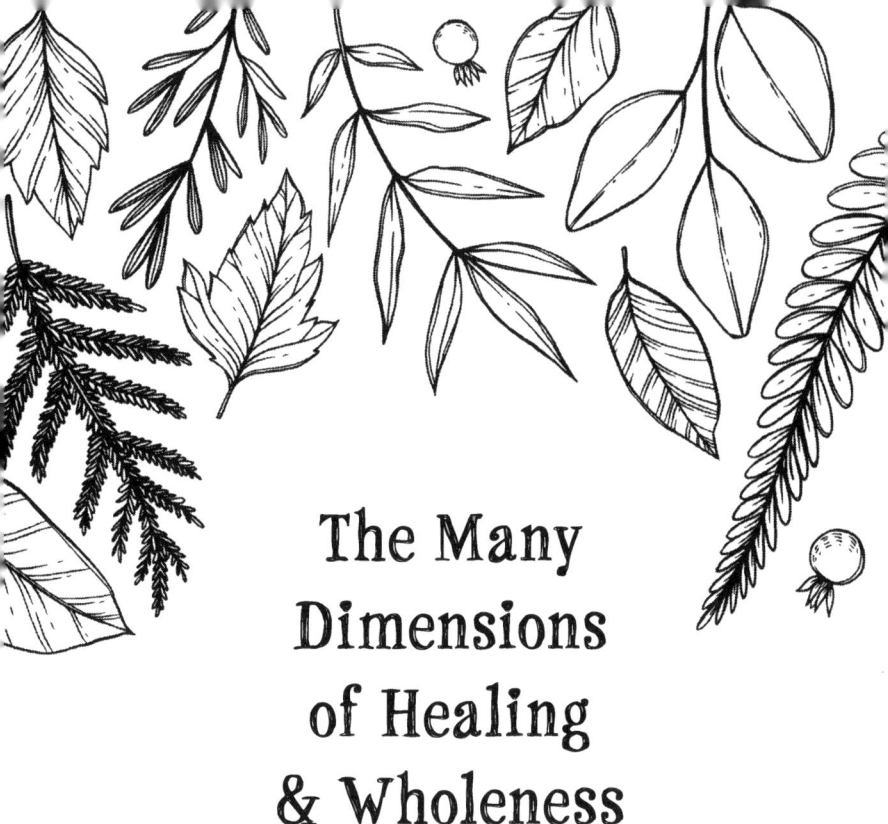

The Many Dimensions of Healing & Wholeness

Christ told us, "I came that they might have life, and have it abundantly" (John 10:10). Healing and wholeness, manifest in abundant living, were at the heart of Jesus' mission. Jesus believed that God's aim for everyone is health and well-being, issuing forth into the world as loving service. He believed that each of us could become an embodiment of God's Spirit, reflecting God's Energy of Love in ways beyond our imagination.

Central to Jesus' message was the affirmation that God is out to love us, not out to get us! God is on the side of health and wholeness, and justice and peace. God does not punish us with sickness and misfortune, nor is God the direct cause of suffering. God challenges whatever—and whomever—stands in the way of experiencing healthy abundance in our personal, relational, and political lives. Those who follow the Way of Jesus support the healing process, wherever it is found, whether in the hospital or laboratory—or the insights of complementary medicine and other religious traditions.

The quest for healing and wholeness is at the heart of the spiritual journey. From the very beginning of religious history, shaman, sage, and priest joined spirituality with the healing of individuals and their communities. Recognizing the holistic nature of life, our spiritual ancestors integrated religion, law, and medicine for the well-being of their communities. Their mission was to bring order out of chaos and restore health to persons and communities.

The concern for healing and wholeness is at the center of the great religious traditions of humankind. The Hebraic prophet and spiritual guide Elijah challenged political leaders to seek justice. He also healed the son of a single mother.

In the Gospels, Jesus proclaimed the coming of God's realm on earth as it is heaven, and he spent his days sharing good news by healing persons in mind, body, and spirit; challenging the ostracism of persons declared "unclean" due to physical and mental health issues, occupation, and ethnicity; and confronting the forces of death with the promise of everlasting life. Gautama Buddha recognized that the lives of most people are characterized by suffering and dissatisfaction, and he provided an Eightfold Path to peace of mind that embraced our occupations as well as our spiritual practices. Chinese sages discovered a lively energy (chi) moving through the Universe and every creature. They believed that maintaining the dynamic balance of universal energy promotes personal and community well-being. First-American spiritual guides nurtured wholeness through achieving harmony with Nature and the nonhuman world, providing rituals to bring well-being to every season of life. Today, we seek wholeness through technological as well as complementary medicine. We respond to disease with meditation and medication, prayer and Prozac.

Healing and wholeness have always been central to my life. As a child, growing up in a Salinas Valley, California, parsonage, I listened with rapt attention to my mother's favorite Sunday afternoon television programs: pioneering televangelist Oral Roberts slapping people on their foreheads as he rebuked spirits of disease; faith healer Kathryn Kuhlman, clothed in a diaphanous gown, whispering, "Be healed"; and evangelist Billy Graham calling people to confess Jesus as their savior, recognizing that the only antidote to death and damnation was a personal relationship with the savior Jesus.

When I left the church as a teenager, I found guidance in the spiritual counsel of American transcendentalists (Ralph Waldo Emerson and Henry David Thoreau), Hindu yogis, and Buddhist monks, along with the countercultural messages of "tune in, turn on, and drop out." My religious life was transformed when I learned Transcendental Meditation at an ashram on the outskirts of the University of California, Berkeley, and then found myself returning to church, having quit drugs and alcohol. At Grace Baptist Church in San Jose, California, I discovered Jesus again for the first time as a spiritual sage and social prophet, whose ministry propelled me to protest the war in Vietnam, seek conscientious objector status, and support the Farm Workers' Movement led by Cesar Chavez and Dolores Huerta. I yearned for spiritual practices to complement my social activism, and during my first university teaching assignment in 1980, I discovered the work of Jerry Jampolsky, who taught Attitudinal Healing to bring about physical and spiritual healing among children with cancer. My encounter with biblical and New Age spiritual affirmations whose goal was to transform mind, body, and spirit opened me to the healing ministry of Jesus. Eventually, I became a healing companion myself through the integration of prayer, traditional Christian laying-on of hands, and Reiki healing touch.

I learned Reiki healing touch, a form of gentle, primarily hands-on energy work aimed at personal and relational wholeness, in the mid-1980s and became a Reiki master/teacher a few years later. For over three decades, I have sought to integrate the teachings of Jesus, Western and global spiritual and medical traditions, and Reiki healing touch for my own healing and wholeness and the healing of persons and the planet. On a daily basis, I am called upon to pray for struggling people and to provide in-person and distant Reiki treatments. (For more on my journey with global healing practices, see *Become Fire! Guideposts for Interspiritual Pilgrims*; *Reiki Healing Touch and the Way of Jesus*; *The Energy of Love: Reiki and Christian Healing*; *God's Touch: Faith, Wholeness and the Healing Miracles of*

Jesus; *Healing Marks: Spirituality and Healing in Mark's Gospel*; and *Healing Worship: Purpose and Practice*.)

As a Christian minister, I have been confronted by the realities of suffering and death. I have felt persons' yearning for healing and wholeness at the descending edges of life. I have experienced the widespread pain and anger brought on by our time of protest and pandemic. My ministry integrates theological reflection, spoken prayers, spiritual affirmations, traditional laying-on of hands, Reiki healing touch, social concern, and, especially during the time of pandemic, intercessory prayer and distant (non-local) healing practices.

As I near my seventh decade in a time of pandemic, healing and wholeness have become central to my spiritual and political involvement. Recognizing my mortality, I seek abundant life, embodied in physical, spiritual, relational, emotional, and intellectual wholeness for the years ahead. When the time comes, I hope to find creative ways to face death with courage and peace of mind. As a pastor facing his own mortality, I have come to believe that when there cannot be a cure, there can always be a healing, a sense of trust in God's love and vision for our future.

I have also recognized that we cannot separate personal from political healing. We need to seek the healing of our nation and the planet. The Earth cries out for healing, and our grand-children's quality of life, including their physical, emotional, and spiritual well-being, depends on our response to the life-destroying realities of global climate change, racism, sexism, economic injustice, and ostracism based on sexual orienta-tion. We cannot be healed persons apart from a healed planet and social order.

A.J. Muste once said, "There is no way to peace; peace is the way." Echoing Muste, Bud-dhist spiritual guide Thich Nhat Hanh counsels that "peace is every step." The same applies to our quest for healing and wholeness. Committing ourselves to be God's companions in healing the Earth, we choose to heal our lives, relationships, and communities.

Healing is imperative in our time of global pandemic and climate change, civil unrest, rac-ism, poverty, and food insecurity. We cannot wait for personal or planetary healing. As the early Christian spiritual guide Paul of Tarsus said, "Now is the day of salvation" (2 Corinthians 6:2). Today is the day we must bring health and heal-ing to our world. We are, as poet June Jordan reminds us, the ones we've been waiting for.

My recognition of the urgency of healing has inspired these *101 Seeds for Healing and Whole-*

ness. Each "seed" provides a guidepost and inspiration for this moment in time, this unrepeatable day fecund with possibilities for healing and transformation. Each seed is intended to invite you to experience healing in the present moment and for the far horizons of your life as you seek to join your personal healing with the spiritual and moral arc of the Universe. Take time each day to breathe deeply, reflect slowly on the words for the day, and carry them with you in your encounters and responsibilities. Living with a sense of healing purpose will transform your life. The seeds of healing will grow into lush foliage, bringing joy to your life and healing to those around you.

SPIRITUAL PRACTICE:
BREATH

On the night of the resurrection, Jesus appeared in an upper room and breathed on his disciples, saying, "Receive the Holy Spirit" (John 20:22). Allan Armstrong Hunter, who was one of my spiritual mentors in graduate school at Claremont, California, similarly counseled us to breathe deeply the Spirit of God in the following way:

I breathe the Spirit deeply in.
And blow it gratefully out again.

Buddhist spiritual teacher Thich Nhat Hanh invites us to find peace moment by moment through mindfulness meditation:

Breathing in I feel calm.

Breathing out I smile.

Breath connects us with our inner resources and the healing energy of the Universe. As we breathe deeply, we experience our connection with creation in all its wondrous diversity.

SPIRITUAL PRACTICE:
LIGHT

The biblical tradition speaks of Christ as the light of the world. Jesus also tells his followers in every age that *we* are the light of the world (Matthew 5:14). Throughout the centuries, light has been identified with healing and wholeness, as well as spiritual illumination that energizes and cleanses our cells and souls.

In this spiritual practice, begin, as you did before, simply by breathing deeply, experiencing your connection with God's Spirit and the world around you with each inhaling and exhaling. Then, after a few minutes, experience God's light entering you with each breath, filling you from head to toe with wisdom, energy, wholeness, and peace. As you exhale, imaginatively share the healing you are experiencing in wider and wider circles of compassion, beginning with your immediate relationships and expanding to your community, nation, and the planet. Experiencing the dynamic interdependence of life, permeated and energized by God's Spirit, you can claim your role as God's companion in healing the world.

May these *101 Souls Seeds for Healing and Wholeness* bring joy, peace, and healing to you and to everyone you encounter. May all creation be blessed with healing and wholeness. This is the day that God has made; let us rejoice and be glad in it!

— Bruce Epperly
The Feast of Epiphany, January 6, 2021

1.

I have come that they might have life,
and have it abundantly.

—JOHN 10:10

We emerge from the original wholeness of God's wise and loving creativity. As Celtic spiritual guide Pelagius asserted, every newborn child reflects the face of God. Amid the challenges of life, we seek—consciously or unconsciously—to experience that original connection with the Divine in ourselves and the world. God is on our side. God's loving energy courses through us, inspiring adventure and healing wounds. God is out to love us, and not hurt us.

Everything God does is aimed at healing and wholeness, beauty, and reconciliation. In quiet moments, we can hear God's heartbeat, the heartbeat of love, beating within our heartbeat and giving us energy to become "healed healers," who share what we have received. Love and mercy. Wholeness and wisdom. Recovery and reconciliation.

God wants you to experience abundant life. God wants creation in all its wondrous diversity to bathe in an abundance of love, creativity, respect, and possibility.

Holy One, Giver of Life and Love, whose energy creates the Universe and heals my life, let me experience Your healing touch and let all creation rejoice in healing and happiness.

2.

The Spirit of the Lord is upon me,
because he has anointed me
to bring good news to the poor.
He has sent me to proclaim release to the captives
and recovery of sight to the blind,
to let the oppressed go free,
to proclaim the year of the Lord's favor.

—LUKE 4:18–19

The world is an amazing place. Yet its beauty contains tragedy. Poverty stunts a child's imagination, crushing hope and initiative. Injustice incarcerates the heart as well as the body,

dimming our spiritual and physical vision, disguising beauty, and encouraging apathy. Walls chain the spirit and malnourish bodies.

Still, Jubilee—the "year of the Lord's favor"—is on the way. Healing springs break through and quench our spiritual thirsts. Walls tumble down, and all creation dances in joyful reconciliation. God's Jubilee year is already here for those who choose to be God's companions in healing the Earth, liberating captives, comforting the grieving, feeding the hungry, and touching lovingly to transform cells and souls.

Descend on me, Spirit. Awaken me to the beauty and wholeness that is my origin and destiny. Show me my vocation as Your healing companion.

3.

Jesus acted to express God's compassion
to people caught up in sin and sickness.

—MORTON KELSEY

One of my spiritual mentors, Episcopalian priest
and theologian Morton Kelséy, describes Jesus'
healing ministry as expansive and holistic. God is
concerned with every aspect of our lives. God is not
far off, sequestered in the unchanging perfection of
a heavenly realm. The realm of God—God's Shalom—is right where we are in the tragic beauty of
aging, physical impairment, political and economic
injustice, as well as compassion, loving energy, sacrifice, and growth. God is the energy of love cours-

ing through all life, the counterforce to disease and division. The inspiration of kindness and caring.

Healing is many-faceted and embraces the whole of life. Nothing is off-limits for God's healing love. No one is outside God's vision of wholeness. Sin and sickness, and division and disease, are never the final word. The final word is Love that creates the Universe, guides the galaxies, inspires the imagination, and awakens us to healing waters flowing through our lives to creation in its wondrous, sometimes chaotic and confused, and always evolving wonder and beauty.

Spirit, empower me be a catalyst for creative transformation and compassionate companionship, so that all my human siblings experience Your delight as they see their own reflection in Your mirror of love.

4.

What do we see in the face
and acts of Jesus that tells us about God?
We see the transforming power
of healing on all levels:
body, emotions, memories, relationships,
decisions, purposes. . . .
And we see that the divine passion and
compassion has never ended
but flows toward us as a limitless,
mighty stream.

—FLORA SLOSSON WUELLNER

Spiritual guide Flora Slosson Wuellner reminds
us that the Love incarnate in Jesus of Naza-

reth is universal in scope and aspiration. Jesus is the embodiment of Divine Energy and Wisdom, Divine Creativity and Compassion. Jesus' incarnation inspires every healing path and supports every faith tradition's quest for wholeness. In Jesus, we experience God's true nature as Love, excluding no one from its concern. The Galilean healer opens us to the ever-flowing streams of wholeness flowing through us toward all creation. Jesus is not far from any of us. He calls us to be "little Christs," even Bodhisattvas, committed to sharing the healing we have received so that all creation will be blessed. We are God's companions on this wondrous journey of love bringing joy to the world so that heaven and nature sing!

Spirit, let me break down the walls that block the flow of Your Energy of Love.

5.

Each of us heals in our own way.
Some people heal because they have work to do.
Others heal because they have
been released from their work
and the pressures and expectations
that others place on them.
Some people need music, others need silence,
some need people around them,
others heal alone.

—RACHEL NAOMI REMEN

Author, physician, and medical school professor Rachel Naomi Remen reminds us that healing takes many forms. There are many paths to healing and wholeness, and many destinations

as well. We can pray for physical healing and the cessation of pain. We may also receive healing that awakens us to the pain of the world, agitating our hearts before comforting our spirits, as we identify with those who experience injustice and intolerance. Our cells may be cured of cancer—or we may flourish despite living with what others perceive as disabilities. We may also fail to experience a physical cure and the healing power of resurrection may take us through the valley of the shadow of death, so that we truly experience what it means to dwell in God's Shalom forever. Let us open to the healing we need in this moment.

Let every moment be a healing moment, Spirit. May I find Your Loving Energy in pain as well as delight, challenge as well as contemplation, protest as well as peace of mind.

6.

Always remember you are braver than you believe,
stronger than you seem, smarter than you think
and twice as beautiful as you'd ever imagined.

—RUMI

Sufi mystic and poet Rumi tells us that we are more than we can imagine. We are star stuff, containing the energy of the Big Bang. We are God's delight, bearing God's energy and creativity. We are Divine vitality, our hearts energized by the Heartbeat of the Universe. We are world shapers. But the path to planetary transforma-

tion begins with the intersection of our spirits with the Spirit of the Universe, which gives birth to us and this wondrous and dynamic Universe.

We are more than we can imagine, and so is everyone else. Divine change moving the Universe bids us to move as well, to grow into people who are more than we can imagine, God's beloved children.

Behold, you are standing on Holy Ground. Behold, you *are* Holy Ground.

Let me be the grace that You have given me. May Your Heart beat within me, making me a child of the Universe and a companion to all creation.

7.

Pythagoras said that
the most divine art was that of healing.
And if the healing art is most divine,
it must occupy itself with
the soul as well as the body;
for no creature can be sound
as long as the higher part is sickly.

—APOLLONIUS OF TYANA

Ancient mathematician, musician, mystic, and medical sage Pythagoras affirmed the whole-person nature of healing. Healing involves the interplay of body, mind, and spirit, but all heal-

ing is ultimately spiritual. It emerges from our inner spirits.

Care for your soul as well as your body. Move your mind as well as your body. Spend time in silence as well as physical exercise. Perhaps even let your movement be meditation, letting Wisdom flow through you as your spiritual cardio charge. Let the healing energy of God inspire each moment and every encounter, transforming your soul as well as your cells.

Let healing abound, Spirit. Let me feed my spirit as well as my body. Move my mind as well as my muscles. Challenge apathy as well as lethargy. Let Your Energy of Love animate every thought, emotion, movement, and relationship.

8.

Health is "a state of well-being and the capability
to function in the state of changing circumstances."
Health is therefore a positive concept
emphasizing social and personal resources
as well as physical capabilities.

—GARY GUNDERSON

Pioneer on the interplay between spirituality, medicine, and society, Gary Gunderson
invites us to see health as multidimensional in
nature. Our health depends on the quality of our
spiritual life, values, relationships, and lifestyle.
It also depends on our ecological, economic, community, and political environment.

Each of us has resources to change our lives and to choose health over sickness and life over death. We also have the resources to create healthy and life-supporting environments, social structures, and public-policy initiatives. This "field" or ecological vision of health reflects the spirit of Jesus' healing ministry, which began with individuals' spiritual and physical health and expanded to include their place in society and religious communities and their economic resources. Holistic health saves lives, deepens spirits, energizes bodies, and transforms nations. The personal is planetary, and the planetary is personal.

Loving Spirit, let me not be content merely with my own health condition. Empower me to work for healthy environments for all Your children.

9.

Jesus said to him,
"Do you want to be made well?"

—JOHN 5:6

Isn't that the key question in life, "Do you want to be well?" Do you want to let go of limitations and seek wholeness? Do you want to let go of the past and awaken to forgiveness and new possibilities in relationships? Do you want to soar despite personal limitations, past trauma, and what others perceive as present disability? There is a force of entropy, of passivity and acceptance

of the status quo; there is also a force that pushes us forward to new horizons of wholeness.

Every moment presents us with choices—for health or illness, agency or passivity, love or fear, life or death. We can choose health and wholeness for ourselves and others. The choice for health changes us and transforms the world.

Loving Spirit, help me to say "yes" to the call of health and healing.

10.

Jesus said to him,
"Stand up, take your mat and walk."
At once the man was made well,
and he took up his mat and began to walk.

—JOHN 5:8-9

Some moments are pivotal. The choice is clear—health or illness, life or death, love or hate, freedom or imprisonment, and agency or passivity. Social activist Angela Davis asserted, "I am no longer accepting the things I cannot change. I am changing the things I cannot accept." In the

story from the Gospel of John, the man at the pool could no longer accept passivity. He could no longer sit on the sidelines of life. He changed what he could no longer accept.

When we choose to be active and to take responsibility, our lives fill with unexpected possibilities. We become actors, creating our own destiny, whether it relates to our personal health, work, and relationships, or as citizens of a planet in need of healing. Stand up. Get in the walk of life. Change the unacceptable and heal the unendurable in the spirit of the Healer from Nazareth.

Loving Spirit, help me stand up and walk. Help me challenge and change the unacceptable.

11.

Elisha sent a messenger to Naaman, saying,
"Go, wash in the Jordan seven times,
and your flesh shall be restored
and you shall be clean."
But Naaman became angry and . . .
he turned and went away in a rage.

—2 KINGS 5:10-12

Naaman expected special treatment. He was angry when Elisha told him that dipping in the nearest stream would cure his skin disease.

There are times when the path to healing is right in front of us: a change in job or diet,

exercise, meditation, discovering our true vocation, reaching out to a companion, learning communication skills. We don't have to do anything dramatic, just follow simple practices that end up changing everything.

Divine providence is always whispering in our ears. Divine light is always guiding our steps. The answers we need are already here, waiting for us to discover, respond, and find the healing we need.

Healing Companion, awaken me to the healing possibilities right in front of me. Let me be attentive to the movements of providence, making a way forward when I perceive a dead end.

12.

Whatever else it means,
the Resurrection of Jesus
suggests that bodies matter to God.
And they ought to matter to us too.

—STEPHANIE PAULSELL

Harvard theology professor Stephanie Paulsell affirms the significance of incarnation and resurrection. Revelation occurs in flesh-and-blood humanity. When scripture says, "God loves the world" (John 3:16), it means that God loves us—body, mind, and spirit. Our bodies matter to God and our health matters to God. God wants us to experience life in its fullness and that means

embracing embodiment, whether in sickness or health.

To recognize that God loves our bodies challenges us to affirm the bodies of others, treating others' bodies with respect. Loving God in the world of the flesh challenges us to treat everyone as a sibling, honoring humanity through ethical relationships. Affirming the bodies of others also means working to ensure that everyone has adequate nourishment, housing, health care, and a healthy environment. Let us rejoice in our embodiment and claim our vocation to nurture the bodies of our siblings.

I thank You, Spirit, for the wonder of embodiment. I commit myself to honor my own body and everyone's body with respect.

13.

Now there was a woman
who had been suffering from
hemorrhages for twelve years. . . .
She had heard about Jesus, and came up
behind him in the crowd
and touched his cloak, for she said,
"If I but touch his clothes, I will be made well."
Immediately . . . she felt in her body
that she was healed of her disease.

—MARK 5:26-30

Many persons suffer from chronic illnesses that will not kill them but limit their activities and make daily life a chore, if not a misery

at times. That is the case in Jesus' healing of the woman with a flow of blood, likely a gynecological illness. She had been sick twelve years, and her sickness rendered her unclean in a society governed by religious purity laws. She was unable to marry and was suspected of contaminating everything she touched. It was even assumed that she was sick due to some moral defect.

The Energy of Love, the power of the Big Bang, chi flowed from Jesus, transforming her cells and soul. Her healing was grounded in the intersection of her faith and God's loving power.

Help me, Spirit, to have faith to respond to my limitations, to passivity, illness, and fear. Let me open to Your ever-present Energy of Love that I might be whole again.

14.

Do you not know that your body
is a temple of the Holy Spirit within you? . . .
Therefore glorify God in your body.

—1 CORINTHIANS 12:19–20

In a time when many persons have poor body images, the early-Christian spiritual guide Paul of Tarsus reminds us that our bodies are holy and amazing. God dwells in every cell, in flowing blood, in respiration, in every breath, and in each firing synapse. We house Divinity. We are temples where God's Spirit may be found. What we do with the temple of God is important. It shapes the quality of our lives and the lives of others.

Glorify God in your body. Give thanks for your body. Eat healthfully and ethically. Touch with love. See your body as an instrument of peace, praising God with every movement, touching holiness with every breath.

Loving Spirit, awaken me to the wonder of my body. Let me use my words, hands, feet, and habits to bring beauty and health to my life and the world.

15.

Let food be thy medicine and
medicine be thy food.

—HIPPOCRATES

The ancient Greek philosopher-physician Hippocrates knew that our diets cure or kill. What we eat and how we eat is a matter of spirituality and ethics as well as nutrition. Our diets shape the quality of our energy and overall well-being. What we eat also contributes to the well-being of others. There is a relationship between our diets and the destruction of Amazon rainforests

and pollution of streams, as well as disease patterns in our nation. We need to live more simply so that others may simply live, as Mahatma Gandhi asserted.

Let us eat mindfully, gratefully, and lovingly, aware of the role of food in our health and the health of others. Let us be God's companions in healing the world by maintaining a "diet for a small planet."

Loving Spirit, let me be mindful of my diet and the relationship of my lifestyle to the well-being of others. I give thanks for those who plant, harvest, process, and deliver my food. I give thanks for this good Earth that nourishes me.

16.

To keep the body in health is a duty. . . .
Otherwise we will not be able
To keep our mind strong and clear.

—GAUTAMA BUDDHA

Have you ever noticed how what you eat or drink immediately shapes your overall well-being? Eating a healthy breakfast can give us the energy to face the day with hope and commitment. Eating too late at night, however, can give us indigestion or keep us awake. Eating too much can make us lethargic, not to mention cause more long-term health problems. Eating is a spiritual enterprise, as Gautama the Enlightened One affirmed.

Eating and drinking are holistic endeavors that shape our spiritual and mental clarity, our ability to make decisions and act on them.

Take some time to reflect on your current diet. Does the food you eat taste good? Do you feel good after your meals? How much, if any, alcohol is appropriate for you to drink and when? Does your dietary lifestyle add beauty or ugliness to the planet? Do you give thanks for persons responsible for your food and do you advocate for just compensation and healthy working conditions for these "essential" employees?

Loving Spirit, thank You for the food I eat, for joyful gatherings, and overall well-being. Let my eating be a blessing for myself and others.

17.

The secret to living well and longer is:
eat half, walk double, laugh triple,
and love without measure.

—TIBETAN BUDDHIST PROVERB

Agood life involves the interplay of order and novelty, tradition and innovation, and predictability and surprise. Eat well but simply. Enjoy what you eat. Move with grace and vigor, for a rolling stone doesn't gather moss, and a moving body inspires an active mind. Rejoice at the wonder of life. Don't take yourself too seriously. (After all, angels fly because they take them-

selves lightly!) Love fully and unconditionally. A good and healthy life involves caring for yourself and reaching out to others. Delight in what you eat, eat with mindfulness, and rejoice in the company you keep.

Help me, Spirit, to live a life of intentionality and spontaneity, welcoming each morning with joy, playing with children, and spreading love wherever I go.

18.

I dislike the thought that some animal
has been made miserable to feed me.

—WENDELL BERRY

Poet, farmer, activist Wendell Berry alerts us to
the ecology of eating. Our food does not magi-
cally appear on our tables but arrives, at least in
most developed countries, through a complicated
chain of relationships from field and farm to
truck, processing plant, and market. We need to
be mindful and grateful: Mindful of the sources
of our food, seeking to eat as nonviolently and
morally as possible, taking into consideration the

people who harvest and butcher our food as well as the lives of the animals we eat. Grateful for the efforts of those who make our meals possible and for the lives of the fish, meat, and poultry we eat.

Recognizing the reality of food insecurity, our approach to eating should embrace generous giving to our kin who struggle to put food on their tables. In mindful gratitude for those who make our food possible, we will add to the joy of life and discover our kinship with all humankind and creation.

Source of Good Things, may my eating be an act of worship and connection. I give thanks for those persons and creatures whose work and sacrifice make it possible for me to enjoy my meals and share with others.

19.

For food in a world where many walk in hunger;
For faith in a world where many walk in fear;
For friends in a world where many walk alone;
We give you thanks, O Lord. Amen.

—AUTHOR UNKNOWN

Spiritual teachers tell us that the most pitiable persons are those who think they can do it on their own, without the support or efforts of others. The self-made person is an illusion, and

holding on to this illusion alienates us from those upon whom our lives depend as well as those who struggle for survival. When we eat our food with gratitude, we go beyond the separation of us-and-them and haves-and-have-nots. We discover that there is no "other." Our hearts expand as we go from individual self-interest to global loyalty. We find ourselves joyfully connected in a world where all are pilgrims and none are strangers.

Heart of the Universe, connect me with the joys and sorrows of humankind and the nonhuman world. Let my life be a blessing to all creation.

20.

The medicine of the future
is going to be prayer and Prozac.

—DALE MATTHEWS

When I was younger, I used to laugh at the plastic pillboxes that my older relatives utilized to ensure they took their daily medications. Now I chuckle at the irony that I have my own personal plastic pillboxes, and my friends and I compare medications, aches and pains, physical-therapy appointments, and upcoming hip and knee replacements! I confess, I don't enjoy living

in the world of medications and CPAP machines, but I have learned that these are also holy.

Spiritual guides counsel us to take our medication in a holy way. We can practice meditation and medication, chanting and chemotherapy, and couple prayer with Prozac and Paxil. Our vitamins and medications, whether pharmaceutical or homeopathic, are gifts from God, intended for our well-being and the well-being of others. We can take them with gratitude, joy, and prayer, making them sacraments of healing for us and others.

Let me surround my medications with meditation and pharmaceuticals with prayer, Spirit.

21.

I think that I cannot preserve
my health and spirits
unless I spend four hours a day at least . . .
sauntering through the woods
and over the hills and fields. . . .
In my walks I return to my senses.

—HENRY DAVID THOREAU

We are made for movement. We are also made for open spaces. Medical studies suggest that a walk outdoors reduces stress, improves cardiovascular function, enhances recovery from surgery, promotes healthy sleep, supports recov-

ery from cancer, combats obesity, and benefits us spiritually as well as emotionally. Walking without purpose, for the pure joy of it, without cell phones and work agendas, restores body, mind, and spirit.

"Go for a walk," philosopher Henry David Thoreau would counsel us. Come to your senses and find God in the great—and small—outdoors.

Loving Spirit, I thank You for movement, open spaces, deep breaths, and time without agendas. Help me make space for my spirit and Your inspiration.

22.

It will be solved in walking.

—AUGUSTINE OF HIPPO

Walking is one of my favorite activities. Many of the words of this book emerged while I was walking on Craigville Beach, near my Cape Cod home. In walking, I bathe my senses in beauty. New and creative ideas come to me. I gain distance from life's problems and often find solutions to personal and professional enigmas.

When you move your body, your thoughts and emotions move as well. You gain novel perspectives. Your imagination is liberated. Take your questions out for a walk. Don't force the issue or try to achieve something immediately. Simply walk and let feelings and thoughts emerge. When you get home or back to your vehicle, you'll have plenty of time to take notes and let your creativity flow. It will be solved in the walking.

Move my feet and move my spirit, Spirit. Let open spaces open my spirit. Let Your wisdom flow in and through me, inspiring me to new ideas and new ways of living.

23.

The sheer act of walking
a complicated path [the labyrinth]—
which discharges energy—
begins to focus the mind. . . .
I feel more focused, more spacious within,
and more responsive to
the people I encounter in my life.

—LAUREN ARTRESS

Overlooking a seaside marsh near our home is a labyrinth I often walk as part of my morning pilgrimage. I usually stop for a few moments to reflect on a question or problem I am facing and then walk gently in the circuitous path to

the center. After a few moments of quiet reflection in the labyrinth's center, I return to my point of departure. On the labyrinth, there is only one path—the way in and the way out are one.

We are all seeking a spiritual center. With spiritual guide Lauren Artress, known for her books on the labyrinth, I find focus, insight, and perspective. Slow contemplative walking centers the spirit, reduces stress, and opens us to deeper wisdom for daily life. In going to the center, we find wisdom for the periphery, and silence as we spiral forth on life's journey.

Let me pause long enough, Spirit, to listen to the deeper wisdom within and without, and be empowered for the challenges of daily life, citizenship, and vocation.

24.

Sanctifying the Sabbath is part
of our imitation of God,
but it also becomes a way to find God's presence.
It is not in space but in time . . .
that we find God's likeness.

—ABRAHAM JOSHUA HESCHEL

According to the Genesis creation stories, the world emerges through the interplay of action and rest. After bringing forth the Universe, God relaxes, enjoying the goodness of creation. According to Jewish mystics, Divine rest is necessary to make room for human creativity. If God

was constantly creating, there would be no room for human freedom and creativity.

Rest allows us to let go of control, let others act, and trust that apart from our efforts, God has the whole world in the Divine hands. When we rest, our souls are replenished, new information is imprinted in our brains, and our bodies recover from the stresses of the day. In resting, we take time to notice the wonders of creation. In pausing, we discover ourselves in the sanctuary of time. Each moment becomes spacious and holy, and life becomes abundant.

Spirit of Creative Wisdom, help me pause, let go of control, and gratefully accept the gifts of life, gaining perspective on the journey that lies ahead for me.

25.

We can cultivate hope through
what I call "Beauty Breaks,"
that is, an intentional excursion
into some form of Beauty at least once a week.

—PATRICIA ADAMS FARMER

Our lives are nurtured by beauty. Yet we often live drab and boring lives, unaware of the wonders right in front of us. Theologian and pastor (and my good friend) Patricia Adams Farmer counsels us to take "beauty breaks." Pause while you're working, doing a chore, posting on social media, and stretch your legs or look out your window, bathing your senses in beauty.

I begin my day by stepping out on my back patio and gazing at the stars, taking in the silence of the predawn as I ponder my place in this vast Universe. While I'm writing or doing preparation for church or teaching, I pause every forty-five minutes for a mini-Sabbath, returning to my backyard, noticing the breeze and the simple beauty of the woods behind our house.

God's grandeur is all-pervasive, in stars and grains of sand, in children's faces and running dogs, in the voices of companions, and in oases of beauty in city streets. Let your soul be well nurtured through beauty breaks.

Artist of the Universe, awaken me to wonder and beauty—and let me be a beauty-bringer wherever I go.

26.

The erotic is that which allows
us deep connection with others,
giving joy, creative energy,
and the capacity for feeling;
that which empowers
persons to change the world;
that which is the deep yes within the self.

—AUDRE LORDE

In today's world, we often have a narrow understanding of the erotic as solely sexual—but
from the time of Plato, eros was also understood
as the Energy of Love that moves life forward

and unites people in loving and learning relationships. Without eros—or passion—no great thing happens. Feminist, poet, civil rights activist, and advocate for Black women's liberation, Audre Lorde affirmed the life-changing power of the erotic that connects, empathizes, creates, and empowers us to transform the world.

What is your passion? What far-off horizon motivates your actions? What gets you up in the morning and enlivens your day? Discovering and then cultivating passion enlightens and enlivens, inspiring and energizing us for each new day.

Loving Spirit, help me discover Your passions in my passions, so that together we might bring joy to the world and beauty to every day.

27.

My beloved speaks and says to me:
Arise, my love, my fair one,
and come away.

—SONG OF SOLOMON 2:10

I often humorously suggest to couples that they take a copy of the Song of Solomon on their honeymoon. God loves bodies and invites us to love God in the world of the flesh. God loves beauty and challenges us to do something beautiful, as Mother Teresa counseled. You can rejoice

and admire beauty, even find passion in beauty, in ways that honor and respect others. Open your eyes to beauty everywhere, especially in your loving relationships, and bring beauty, delight, and joy to those with whom you are intimate. God blesses healthy intimacy everywhere.

Help me, Spirit, to love those around me, body, mind, and spirit. Let my actions add to their health, beauty, and delight.

28.

This is the day that God has made
and I will rejoice and be glad in it.

—PSALM 118:24

Physician and philosopher Larry Dossey claims that one of the most serious issues confronting people today is "hurry sickness." Like the White Rabbit from *Alice's Adventures in Wonderland*, we often perceive ourselves as "late, late for a very important date," even though our schedule is often of our own making. Many retirees, or persons with flexible schedules like myself, create stress trying to live up to unnecessary expectations and optional appointments. We feel rushed when in

fact we often have "all the time in the world."

The psalmist reminds us that today is a day of wholeness and joy. A day of gratitude and jubilee in which God woke us up to innumerable possibilities for love, companionship, creativity, and rest. We can rejoice in this day, prioritize our schedule, and let go or deemphasize what is unimportant. In this Holy Here and Now, we will fulfill our responsibilities with grace and calm, soothing those around us by the spaciousness of our attitudes and bringing peace to stressful situations.

Holy One, let me see time as spacious and holy, an opportunity to create, reflect, and serve, knowing that in this "thin place," where time and eternity meet, I have all the time I need to do something beautiful for You and my neighbor and family.

29.

When we pray for inner healing,
we are really asking Jesus . . .
to bring healing to the distressing
and painful memories of the past.
. . . We need to take him [who is love]
into the places where there was no love.

—RUTH CARTER STAPLETON

We are often trapped in the past. We experience the limitations of past failures; the trauma of painful encounters in childhood; and alienation from friends, family, and organizations that have caused us harm. At such moments we need spiritual and emotional healing that comes

from knowing we are not alone, and that Jesus or Buddha or another spiritual teacher or dear friend walks with us, providing protection and love.

God is with us. Christ walks beside us. Often God comes to us also in the form of trusted friends, pastoral caregivers, or mental health professionals. Sometimes we may even need medication to calm our spirits, remembering that medication, like meditation, is a gift from God. Help is on the way! Nothing can separate us from the love of God.

Spirit of Healing and Wholeness, be with me as I face the pain of trauma. Soothe my spirit, strengthen my resolve to heal. Remind me that You are with me and that You are sending healing persons into my life. Thank You for being with me in darkness as well as light.

30.

Do not be conformed to this world,
but be transformed
by the renewing of your minds.

—ROMANS 12:2

Healing involves a commitment to constant transformation. The world of alienation, consumerism, and possessiveness often limits our sense of possibility. It values privilege, power, victory, and punishment. God's world is that of constant creative transformation, and of wider circles of love and healing. God's love takes us beyond the binary us-them, in-out, friend-enemy, as it pushes us toward the horizons of personal

and planetary healing and wholeness.

Still, there are moments when transformation and renewal elude us. There are times when we cannot forgive those who harass, traumatize, and abuse, whether in ministry, family, or politics. We need to leave forgiveness to God when we can't forgive someone whose actions still distress us. We need to trust God with the spiritual and moral arcs of history when we can't move them forward ourselves due to our own fatigue, burnout, or trauma. Still, God is at work in our lives to bring healing and wholeness and give us the grace we need to grow in and through life's challenges.

Loving Spirit, help me commit myself to a life of renewal and creative transformation. You will make a way for me when I perceive no way forward.

31.

Three times I appealed to the Lord about this,
that [this ailment] would leave me,
but he said to me, "My grace is sufficient for you,
for power is made perfect in weakness."

—2 CORINTHIANS 12:9-10

There are times that, despite our best efforts, our health condition remains unchanged. We remain troubled in body, mind, and spirit. At such moments, we must call on a Power and Wisdom greater than our own. We throw ourselves into the loving arms of God in the same way that

as children we reached out to a loving adult. We open to God's Energy of Love to receive the healing and wholeness for which we yearn . . . and the patience to deal with what cannot be changed.

This is not a retreat from agency, but a recognition that when we have reached our limits, the Spiritual Power of the Universe is still at work, nurturing us, holding us up, and making a way where we see no way. Our strength comes from our partnership with God and not our rugged individualism. When we open to God's Power, we gain new insight, inspiration, and integrity for the journey ahead. God's grace is enough.

Loving Spirit, help me to trust Your wisdom and grace.

32.

A new heart I will give you,
and a new spirit I will put within you;
and I will remove from your body
the heart of stone
and give you a heart of flesh.

—EZEKIEL 36:26

Apathy breeds hardheartedness. Apathy dead-ens our spirits to the pain of others. We believe that the suffering of children separated from their parents does not concern us. The deaths of homeless persons on American streets are unim-portant to us.

To be healthy, our apathetic spirits need to be broken and healed. Our hard hearts need to be softened. To find healing, our hearts need transformation from apathy to empathy. We need to have the doors of perception cleansed, so that we can experience the pain of others. We need to have our hearts melted, so we can honor our unity with all life. A heart of flesh is open to the world's pain. In that openness, we also experience great joy and solidarity with all creation.

Break my hardheartedness, Spirit, that I may feel the pain—and joy—of those around me.

33.

You are the light of the world. . . .
Let your light shine before others.

—MATTHEW 5:14, 16

These words from Jesus' Sermon on the Mount are some of the most important words in scripture. First, they affirm who you are and banish any lack of self-esteem. You shine like Jesus. (See John 1:1–5, 9.) Second, the light within you gives you a vocation: to let your light shine. Your decisions can change the world. Your light can help others find their way and discover the life-

changing Presence of God. Be a light to yourself, as Gautama Buddha counseled his followers, and then let your light shine!

Let me see the light in myself and all creation, Light-Giver. Let me be a light-giver in Your image, showing Your light to others.

34.

The dying, . . . the unwanted, the unloved—
they are Jesus in disguise. . . .
We have so much to learn from them.

—MOTHER TERESA

Health and wholeness are a matter of perception—a matter of seeing the Divine in
yourself and others. When the doors of perception
are opened, as William Blake affirmed, every
face will be a portal to infinity. Everyone will
be Christ in disguise. We will not be separate or

superior. Our goal will be to give and receive a blessing and healing in every encounter. We will recognize that the vulnerable and impoverished are our teachers, inspiring our spiritual growth and expanding our compassion. We will honor our unity with every person and all creation.

Spirit of All Creation, give me a compassionate heart. Free me from binary separation from my kin. Let me see you, O Spirit, in every face. Let every encounter inspire me to bless and be blessed.

35.

Do you know what you are?
You are a manuscript of a divine letter.
You are a mirror reflecting a noble face.
This universe is not outside of you.
Look inside yourself;
everything that you want,
you are already that.

—RUMI

Sufi mystic Rumi proclaims our inherent nobility and invites us to embark on a journey of self-discovery. We cannot be whole unless we embrace ourselves in our grandeur as well as our

imperfection. The self we seek is dynamic, multi-dimensional, and constantly growing. Divine energy flows in and through you. Opening to God's energy within us widens and deepens our lives and gives us perspective on life's challenges.

Look inside yourself. Listen to your evolving life. Embrace your connectedness with all creation. And then, let your life speak!

Spirit, let Your life enliven, enlighten, and energize me. Let me experience my grandeur as well as my imperfection, trusting that You have a vision of greatness for me.

36.

God to enfold me, God to surround me,
God in my speaking, God in my thinking.
God in my sleeping, God in my waking . . . ,
God in my life, God in my lips,
God in my soul, God in my heart.

—CELTIC PRAYER FROM
THE *CARMINA GADELICA*

When there can't be a cure, there can always be healing. Healing ultimately involves the experience of peace, regardless of life's circumstances. Peace emerges from a sense of God's Presence in all the seasons of life, reminding us

that our lives are part of a never-ending story of God's creative love for us and the Universe. God's love brought us into life, guides our steps, and surrounds us with grace. God inspires our words and meditations. God's love receives our lives at the moment of death, inviting us to share in further adventures of creative wisdom and beauty.

Forever surrounding, inspiring, and energizing me, O Spirit, let me live with grace, courage, peace, and joy, letting Your wisdom and love flow in me and through me to all the world.

37.

Healing begins where the wound was made.

—ALICE WALKER

No one's childhood is ever perfect. From the very beginning, despite our original wholeness as God's beloved children, we also experience the imperfection of our world, mediated to us through our families of origin, community, political environment, and responses to our actions. Even a happy childhood has pain and woundedness.

Author Alice Walker shows us that within the wound is the possibility of healing. Denial of suffering and woundedness leads to more pain

or, perhaps, spiritual and emotional anesthesia. Openness to our childhood and adult wounds is an open door to self-awareness and agency in the healing process. God is at work in our wounds as well as our joys to bring us new and abundant life. No wound is ultimate. All wounds contain an antidote that enables us to experience new possibilities growing as soul seeds out of the humus of pain.

Giver of Abundant Life, let me experience blessing amid limitation and healing in woundedness. Let me open to Your desire for my wholeness and the paths toward health You set before me. Give me patience with the process and hope for the healing.

38.

We delight in the beauty of the butterfly,
but rarely admit the changes it has gone through
to achieve that beauty.

—MAYA ANGELOU

Life is change. The early Greek philosopher Heraclitus of Ephesus proclaimed that all things flow and that you cannot step in the same waters twice. (An upstart student corrected his teacher, saying you can't even step into the same waters once!) With the flow of life comes novelty and also the reality of pain. The Universe, manifest in our personal growth, will not let us stand

still. Letting go is a necessity, whether we like it or not. Think of all the changes since your conception. Think of the changes that lie ahead.

Not all change is positive; aging brings physical diminishment and the loss of roles and relationships. Still, within all change lies holy possibility. Change brings fear—and it also brings hope, beauty, creativity, and wonder. Let us face change, trusting the journey of the butterfly.

Spirit of Change and Glory, give me Your grace as I ponder the future. Let me embrace mystery and what is unknown with hope and courage and agency.

39.

May all beings everywhere
plagued with sufferings of body and mind
quickly be freed from their illnesses.
May those frightened cease to be afraid,
and may those bound be free.
May the powerless find power.

—BUDDHIST HEALING PRAYER

Each of us is a Bodhisattva or Christ in the making. Jesus and Gautama both affirmed an open Universe in which their lives were inspirations and examples for our own spiritual evolution. Jesus is my healer and guide, and the

object of my spiritual devotion, not because he hoards salvation or proclaims his distance from me, but because he presents a vision, inspiration, and energy for my own unique embrace of God's love in my life. Buddha wants us to be saved, and Jesus wants us to be enlightened. Though paths and practices may differ, both want us to be fully human, and thus fully enlightened and divine.

Let us embrace the light by praying for the wholeness of all creation and all God's human children, seeing holiness in the weak as well as the strong, the loving as well as the defensive, friend as well as foe.

Let all creatures find happiness, Spirit, and let me by my actions bring beauty to this good Earth and its creatures.

40.

May all beings be peaceful.
May all beings be happy.
May all beings be safe.
May all beings awaken to
the light of their true nature.
May all beings be free.

—BUDDHIST LOVINGKINDNESS PRAYER

In the spirit of the Buddhist lovingkindness prayer, I often pause for a few minutes to breathe deeply God's healing and loving light, experiencing my body as light-filled. I breathe in

the dynamic, interdependent, creative, and loving energy of God. As I exhale, I let my breath bring life and peace to those in my immediate environment, the community, the nation, and the planet.

We are one and our spirits are joined in God's Beloved Community in which the joy of others deepens my joy, and my joy adds to their beauty of life. Joined in one Great Breath, we are one in spirit and embodiment in all our diversity. Our peace is one. Joining unity and diversity brings appreciation and cooperation, and the world is blessed.

Let me awaken to beauty and love, Spirit.
Let each breath be a prayer, connecting me
with my neighbor and healing the Earth.

41.

As soon as healing takes place,
go out and heal somebody else.

—MAYA ANGELOU

We are intended to be "healed healers." Every blessing we receive blesses others. We give what we have received and receive when we give. Our healings are intended to be catalysts for others. We are part of an intricate ecology of healing. Intertwined in a fabric of relationships, what happens to us shapes the world around us—and the world around us also shapes our experience.

Let your moments of healing radiate out into the Universe, blessing and being blessed in the wondrous healing circle of life.

Thank you, Healing Spirit, for my experiences of healing. Let me share my healings in ways that inspire and promote the healing of others.

42.

Reiki means Universal Life Energy.
And we are composed of this energy.
Everyone can use this energy for healing.

—HAWAYO TAKATA

Reiki is prayer with your hands, one that I have integrated with my Christian prayer life. As I touch someone or give a distant treatment, similar to intercessory prayer, I feel a sense of connection with them as the healing energy of the Universe joins us. Reiki healing flows, but it is also always here waiting for us to notice.

If you aren't trained in a healing modality, such as Reiki, therapeutic touch, or medical qigong, you can still touch yourself and others with love, knowing that loving touch heals and connects.

We live in an energetic Universe in which the Energy of Love—the flowing chi and Divine creativity—energizes our own bodies, minds, spirits, and relationships, just as it also brought forth the Big Bang, spun galaxies, and slowly evolved our planet. Connected to the energy of the Universe, we experience health and well-being. Disconnected, we spiritually, emotionally, physically, and relationally wither.

Let Your loving energy flow in, from, and through me, Spirit, to transform the world.

43.

Just for today, do not worry.
Just for today, do not be angry.
Honor your teachers,
your neighbors, your friends.
Give thanks for all living things.
Earn your living honestly.

—MIKAO USUI

Mikao Usui reminded his Reiki healing touch students that healing is a moral enterprise that touches every aspect of our lives. Any moment can be a healing moment. As Usui notes,

our trust in the healing energy of the Universe calms our spirits, enables us to live peacefully, inspires respect for the people who have shaped our lives, connects us in gratitude with all creation, and compels us to live with integrity.

Every moment is important. Every encounter is sacred. When one moment is joyful or healed, the Universe experiences wholeness. Let our hands, words, and relationships all bring beauty to the world, welcome to outsiders, and healing to the planet, one moment at a time.

Remind me, Spirit, that my life can heal the world. Unimportant as I may seem, I make a difference. Countless acts of kindness and healing tip the balance from death to life and hate to love.

44.

When we speak of inner healing,
we refer to the experience
in which the Holy Spirit
restores health to the deepest area of our lives
by dealing with the root cause
of our hurts and pain.

—RUTH CARTER STAPLETON

God's light shines in the darkness of the past, healing our memories and past traumas. In places of pain, we can ask God to be our companion. In the darkest valley, God is with us, prepar-

ing a table for us, anointing us with oil, giving us an ever-flowing cup of love, and surrounding us with goodness and mercy (Psalm 23).

Visualize God being with you in a place of pain. Experience God's loving arms—perhaps in terms of Jesus, Buddha, or a First American medicine person—surrounding, protecting, and healing. You are safe, you are loved, you are healed. Nothing can ever separate you from the loving care of God.

Let me open to healing of the past as I also open to the future, Spirit. You are with me, every step of the way, healing memories and enlivening possibilities for the future.

45.

I looked for God.
I went to a temple
and I didn't find God there.
Then I went to a church
and I didn't find God there.
Then I went to a mosque
and I didn't find God there.
Then finally I looked in my heart
and there God was.

—RUMI

During the time of pandemic, many people were worried about canceling in-person worship services. In my own congregation, while we seldom

saw each other in the flesh, our church experienced an amazing closeness on Zoom and expanded its outreach to the larger community. We discovered that God was in our hearts and in our community.

The traditional doctrine of "omnipresence" means that God is present everywhere and in everyone. Deep down, God is in all of us. Wherever we are, God is present. The heartbeat of God beats in our heartbeat. God breathes with our lungs. God inspires our thoughts.

Look in your heart and you will find holiness—and then discover it everywhere.

Let me look deeply in my heart and find You there, Spirit. Not confined by building or creed, ritual or tradition, Your love is ever new in every life.

46.

Blessing provides the leverage
that changes the way we view the world.
It is something we can receive.
It is something we can give away.

—GARY GUNDERSON

Blessing surrounds others with compassion, energy, and love. Blessing upbuilds, strengthens, and empowers those around us. Blessing exponentially expands love in our world. Blessing connects and heals (while cursing divides and destroys).

When we live a life of blessing, every moment is freighted with beauty. Every moment is Spirit-filled. Every encounter places us on holy ground.

Bless the world, O my soul. Bless this day, my work, play, meals, and relationships. Bless all whom I meet. Spirit, may Your blessings flow bountifully through me.

47.

Grant that I may become beautiful within
and that my inner and outer life be one.
May I see true wealth in terms of wisdom.
May I live simply and have no more
than is right for me to possess.

—PLATO

The philosopher Plato guides our path to beauty, reminding us of the interplay of inner and outer beauty. Integrity is the virtue that joins our inner and outer lives. We walk the talk and talk the walk. We are committed to healing

and justice in private, when no one is looking, and in public, when our lives are on display. We prize wisdom over possession and compassion over power. Beauty shines from us regardless of our age and health condition. A beautiful soul is a large soul able to embrace variety, diversity, contrast, without losing its center. A beautiful soul plants seeds of beauty everywhere. These seeds sprout, grow, and nourish everyone around us.

Loving Spirit, let me place integrity at the heart of my life. Let me cultivate inner beauty and share that beauty with everyone I meet.

48.

Prayer is a genuinely non-local event—
that is, it is not confined to a specific space
or a specific moment in time.
Prayer reaches outside the here-and-now;
it operates at a distance
and outside the present moment.

—LARRY DOSSEY

Prayer is nonlocal, as physician-philosopher Larry Dossey asserts. Our prayers radiate across the Universe, without consideration of space or time. When I pray, I create a field of force around those for whom I pray, bringing

greater energy to their lives, orienting them toward wholeness, and opening the door for a greater influx of Divine activity to heal, empower, and support.

We can never fully understand the mechanics of prayer. But we can pray—about things large and small, past and future. In prayer, we surround others with words, light, and love, joining one another in God's arc of healing. So let us pray often, with and without words, committing ourselves and others to God's loving care.

Teach me, Spirit, to pray in a way that fits my faith and life situation. Let me be patient with prayer, blessing all creation and leaving past, present, and future in Your care.

49.

Some people want to recognize God
in some pleasant enlightenment—
then they get pleasure and enjoyment
but not God.

—MEISTER ECKHART

German mystic Meister Eckhart reminds us that although we hope to glide down Easy Street, the times of greatest spiritual growth often occur when we are meandering down bumpy roads, trying to navigate around potholes.

God does not cause the suffering we experience. God is not the cause of cancer, car accidents,

abuse, or injustice. Still, God works through these and makes a way when there is no way. In difficult times, we discover our need to seek the assistance of others. And then, when we discover we can't make it on our own, God makes a way, placing caring persons and new insights into our lives.

When we can't find a cure, when we are confronted by our mortality, we need to look for God's healing presence within the struggle. In life and death, God is our companion and inspiration. Wounds can be windows into Divinity.

Waymaker Spirit, help me to accept the totality of my life as an opportunity for growth.

50.

Pray without ceasing.

—1 THESSALONIANS 5:17

A spiritual guide once said that the spiritual life is a matter of constantly falling down and getting back up again. Prayerfulness does not prevent us from slipping into old habits, becoming annoyed or anxious. It does, however, help us return to our spiritual center when we have taken the wrong path, behaviorally, relationally, or spiritually. Prayer is at the heart of the healing journey. It is both preventative and responsive to the challenges we face. Prayer is an intention and attitude, not restricted to words or rituals. Every breath can be a prayer.

My own prayerfulness involves a rhythm of contemplative silence that leads to prayerful action. My day begins with meditation. During the day, I pause to take my spiritual pulse, noting my emotional and spiritual state, and reorienting my spiritual GPS if necessary; throughout the day, I pause to breathe deeply. I take note of any events that need me to respond with love in action. My goal is to be attentive to God in all the moments of life, constantly returning to my spiritual depths as the foundation for creative and contemplative activism.

Throughout the day, may I open to Your gentle Spirit, guiding my words and actions. When I falter, challenge me to return to my spiritual center so that I may serve You and bring healing to the world.

51.

God is a circle whose center is everywhere
and whose circumference is nowhere.

—ST. BONAVENTURE

It is more important to ask, "What kind of God do you believe in?" than "Do you believe in God?" The God in whom I believe is present in every moment of experience. God is the dynamic ground of my being, the creative source of everyone else's being. I am at the center of God's love, and so is everyone else. God experiences my life

and every other life from the inside and not just as an observer. No one is outside the center. No place is God-forsaken. No season of life is without God's presence. I can be confident that wherever I go, I am in God's care. I can be confident that in the heights and depths of life, God is with me. Every place is home, and every path leads home, for God is a circle whose center is everywhere and whose circumference is nowhere.

Circle me with love, O Spirit. Circle me with grace, Holy Companion. Let me see You in myself and in everyone.

52.

I mean the stature of a person's soul,
the range and depth of his love,
his capacity for relationships . . .
the strength of your spirit
to encourage others to become freer
in the development of
their diversity and uniqueness . . .
the magnanimity of
concern to provide conditions
that enable others to increase in stature.

—BERNARD LOOMER

The Gospels proclaim that "Jesus grew in wisdom and stature and favor with God and human-

kind" (Luke 2:52). In times of pandemic and protest, division and dishonesty, we need to be persons of stature who can embrace political, economic, ethnic, and racial diversity in our increasingly polarizing age. We need to go beyond binary division to seek holistic unity. We need to have the largeness of soul to treat our opponents with the same care as we give to those for whom we advocate. We need to commit ourselves to constantly enlarging our spirits, so that no person is foreign and every place is our spiritual home. Let us pray that we be "mahatmas" or great souls, let us seek to be little Christs, who share God's blessings with all creation.

Spirit, give me a big soul. Give me spiritual stature large enough to embrace diversity and heal division.

53.

The healing of purpose for Jesus and for us
is to decide to live in God's present and presence.
The healing of purpose
seems to involve a naming . . .
to fulfill the potential of
God's purpose for our lives.

—JOHN BIERSDORF

There are as many purposes as there are persons—and each season of life has unique purposes, just as each moment is meaningful. When we are living according to our God-given purpose, our lives have meaning for ourselves, our neighbors, and the planet. Indeed, our purposes are

part of God's larger purposes for our time and place and for the future our actions shape. Our purposes may keep us at home, caring for grand-children and children, helping our community flourish, or sustaining an organization. They also may challenge us to pick up our luggage and hit the road. When we take our gifts to God in prayer, God guides our path, showing us our calling and directing us toward the people who need our care.

What gets you up in the morning? What is the passion that energizes you? What horizons call you toward greatness, and toward becoming your best self? What is your Great Work?

Spirit of the Far Horizon, reveal to me Your purposes for me. Help me align myself with them, and enable me to creatively make them my own.

54.

There are all different kinds of voices
calling you to all different kinds of work,
and the problem is to find out
which is the voice of God. . . .
The place God calls you to is the place
where your deep gladness
and the world's deep hunger meet.

—FREDERICK BUECHNER

Our vocation emerges from the interplay of our gifts and the world's needs. Our passions need direction, and the world provides a pathway

for living out our callings. Providence moves through our lives, placing us where we need to be and giving us opportunities to make a difference in the world as well as grow our souls. Wholeness comes from listening to our lives prayerfully, and then, out of that listening, letting our lives speak in joyful and passionate self-discovery and service to those around us.

Loving Spirit, let me listen deeply for my calling—and emerging callings—and then share my life with others for Your glory and the healing of the planet.

55.

At some moment I did answer Yes to Someone,
or Something, and from that hour
I was certain that existence is meaningful
and that, therefore, my life,
in self-surrender, had a goal.

—DAG HAMMARSKJOLD

When we say "yes" to the Voice of God, everything changes. Turning to God's vision, even if the Holy comes to us unnamed and unknown, opens us to new energies and possibilities. A way is made. People come into our lives. Resiliency and resolve emerge. We become more whole.

When I said "yes" to being part of the "101 Soul Seeds" series, I felt a healthy avalanche of creative ideas pushing me forward toward my goal. Saying "yes" to love, saying "yes" to justice, saying "yes" to agency—it changes the circumstances of our lives and our impact on the world. When we say "yes" to life each morning, our days will be filled with energy, beauty, discovery, and adventure. Healed from apathy, aimlessness, and boredom, we will bring joy to the world!

Help me, Spirit, to say "yes" to life, love, and joy. Help me to say "yes" to adventure and open myself to unexpected energy and possibility.

56.

[To prepare for a Vision Quest]
the first thing a person must do is to pray. . . ,
affirming "my relationship and my dependence
upon the Creator and the spirits.
Everything they show me is for my spiritual growth
and the peoples' welfare."

**—WILLIAM WALK SACRED,
CREE NATION SPIRITUAL GUIDE**

While the Vision Quest, practiced by many North American indigenous peoples, is a rite of passage specific to indigenous cultures, its wisdom is found in every religious quest. The

participant, often on the cusp of adulthood, goes on a spiritual journey to seek wisdom, power, and vocation from guiding Spirits. At every time of change, we need to seek a vision to guide our next steps and open us to new possibilities and the energy to embody them. At the beginning of his ministry, Jesus went to the wilderness to pray. Buddha sat under the Bo Tree to seek enlightenment. In times of change, a vision quest enables us to listen to the voice of God. The quest frees us from the voices of our culture and our temptation to conform to others' visions rather than our own deepest wisdom.

Spirit of Life, grant me a vision. Show me the next steps of my journey. Give me a glimpse of the far horizon that lies ahead for me.

57.

You can pray until you faint,
but unless you get up and try to do something,
God is not going to put it in your lap.

—FANNIE LOU HAMER

Protest and pray, so counsels civil rights activist and feminist pioneer Fannie Lou Hamer. Our prayers are ineffectual, Hamer believed, unless we complete them with hands and feet. Our prayers are intended to change who we are and transform our priorities. The immediate

impact of prayer may be to get us off our couches and into the real world to work for justice. Prayer is completed when our words take wings, inviting us to imagine a different world for us and our communities, and then take hands and feet to work for that world.

As you pray, visualize how you can be part of God's vision of healing. What actions can you take to amend your behaviors and values to bring wholeness to your life, family, and community?

Loving Spirit, let my prayers inspire me to change my heart, emphathize more deeply those in pain, and find guidance in addressing the suffering of our planet.

58.

Solitude is for me a fount of healing
which makes my life worth living.
Talking is often a torment for me,
and I need many days of silence
to recover from the futility of words.

— CARL JUNG

Pioneering psychiatrist Carl Jung points out the importance of silence in the healing process. While Jung's orientation may be more introverted than some of us experience, there is a virtue in stillness. Time spent in prayer and

meditation. Retreat and pilgrimage. Times of silence enable us to hear the deeper voices of our own spirits as well as the Divine Spirit. Out of silence grow seeds of personal transformation, wisdom, creativity, and action.

Appropriate to your life circumstances, consider devoting a portion of every day to solitude. Examine your words and speech. Do they bring wholeness and justice? Do they improve the world around you? If your schedule permits, take more extended times for solitude on a weekly, monthly, or yearly basis.

Spirit, teach me to be still and know
Your Presence. Let my stillness calm my
spirit and awaken me to Your voice and
my deepest wholeness.

59.

Knowing your own darkness is the best method
for dealing with the darkness of other people.
One does not become enlightened
by imagining figures of light,
but by making the darkness conscious. . . .
Your visions will become clear
only when you can look into your own heart.

—CARL JUNG

Jung sees darkness as neither positive nor negative. It is the neglected part of the self, the shadow often hidden by everyday consciousness. It is the "dark side" of violence and alienation that plagues even saints.

Jesus went on a retreat in the wilderness to face his temptations and discern his vocation. Like Jesus, we need to find safe and creative ways to uncover the hidden parts of ourselves. Such investigations are an invitation to a holy adventure. In discovering the "many selves" that live beneath consciousness, we can both heal their pain and gain from their insight and energy. Darkness has a light of its own. God is working within the unconscious to bring healing to our whole lives. In accepting the unconscious, we gain power for our conscious life and healing in our relationships.

Loving Spirit, help me face the unknown in myself with grace and courage. Let Your light shine in the darkness, giving me strength for the journey of self-discovery.

60.

Where can I go from your spirit?
Or where can I flee from your presence? . . .
If I say, "Surely the darkness shall cover me
and the light around me become night,"
even the darkness is not dark to you;
the night is as bright as the day,
for darkness is as light to you.

—PSALM 139:7–8, 11–12

God is with me in light and darkness. God embraces my elation and despair. God knows my virtues and vices, my public achievements

and my private anxieties. Even in the deepest darkness, God is with me, shedding light into the darkness, helping me find a way.

In the darkness, look for the glimmer of Divine light. Even the smallest ray of light may lead you to a therapist, spiritual guide, or intimate friend. It may bring synchronous encounters or unexpected insights. It may guide you to medication as well as meditation. The darkness of chaos and disease cannot overwhelm the light. God's light within and around you moves toward healing. God wants you to be whole.

In the darkness, shed Your light, O Spirit. Help me know You are with me. Help me find my way.

61.

Grace strikes us when we
are in great pain and restlessness.
It strikes us when we
walk through the dark valley
of a meaningless and empty life. . . .
It is as though a voice were saying:
"You are accepted. . . .
Do not try to do anything now. . . .
Simply accept the fact that you are accepted!"

—PAUL TILLICH

German-American theologian Paul Tillich describes the moment of grace when we feel accepted in our wondrous imperfection and

tragic beauty. A Power and Wisdom greater than ourselves embrace our wholeness and invite us to embrace the totality of our lives as well. God accepts us. God loves us. God knows who we are, the hero and villain, the saint and sinner, the social activist and apathetic bystander. God knows us, works to heal us, and most of all accepts and blesses us.

Spirit of Grace and Glory, let me accept Your grace, embrace Your love, and welcome Your healing. Thank You for loving me, and give me the grace to accept others as You have accepted me.

62.

The body is a self-healing organism,
so it's really about clearing things out of the way
so the body can heal itself.

—BARBARA BRENNAN

Our bodies aim at wholeness, according to energy healer Barbara Brennan. There is a moral and spiritual arc in the Universe aiming toward justice and wholeness. There is also an arc toward healing within our bodies, minds, and spirits. God's energy flows through us seeking our wholeness.

Often, we block the healing energy of the Universe through lifestyle, diet, attitudes, or behaviors. This blockage may also have its origin in

systemic injustice, poverty, racism, and unhealthy family environments, as well as physical issues. Still, regardless of our personal or social situation, the healing Presence of God flows in and through us, activating forces of wholeness within the limits of our current health condition. We tap into this graceful energy of wholeness in many ways: prayer, meditation, energy work (Reiki, therapeutic touch, qigong, Tai Chi), affirmations, exercise, and diet. Each enhances the forces of healing within us so that we can live abundantly and share creatively with our communities.

Spirit, let me tap into the movements toward healing in my body, mind, and spirit. Let me open to healing light in my cells and soul—and out of my healing, share healing with others.

63.

Give us courage to change what must be altered,
serenity to accept what cannot be helped,
and the insight to know the one from the other.

—REINHOLD NIEBUHR

Many of us have benefitted from the Serenity Prayer, based on a poetic prayer initially written in the 1930s by theologian Reinhold Niebuhr. It teaches us that among the many paths of healing is our response to what we cannot change. This might be a sibling struggling with mental health issues, the pain and debilitation of our own chronic illness, caring for a spouse with Alzheimer's disease, having to move to assisted living, or facing an incurable illness.

My father's pastor told me of an encounter with my dad, a nursing home resident following a debilitating stroke. My dad looked up at him with a wry smile and mumbled, "I'm stuck but it's okay." Sometimes, healing means being "okay" in a difficult time, feeling Divine presence when we are out of human-made options. Knowing God is with us and that nothing in life and death can separate us from God's love—that is healing! The problem may not be solved, the illness may not be cured, but we continue walking with faith in the ultimate goodness of God and the meaningfulness of our lives. This is the ground of peace. It's the peace that passes all understanding—knowing that we are loved into life and loved into eternity.

Give me peace of mind, Spirit, that allows me to awaken each day with faith, hope, and love.

64.

The outside world told black kids
when I was growing up
that we weren't worth anything.
But our parents said it wasn't so,
and our churches and our schoolteachers
said it wasn't so.
They believed in us,
and we, therefore, believed in ourselves.

—MARIAN WRIGHT EDELMAN

The healing of persons and communities goes hand in hand. Educator and advocate for children Marian Wright Edelman recognizes that

resilience—staying power in facing adversity—comes through a community's countercultural vision. All children need at least one adult who helps them see their value and claim the Great Work toward which God calls them. All children—and all adults—need someone who believes in them; who sees their deeper beauty and giftedness, and then helps them embody their dreams. Others' healing words and attitudes show us our deepest nature and then invite us to live out our dreams.

What words do you need to hear? With whom do you need to share words of wholeness and possibility?

Let me see in myself what You see in me, Spirit, and let me be the visionary for others, inviting them toward Your greatness in their lives.

65.

Set me as a seal upon your heart,
. . . for love is strong as death,
passion fierce as the grave. . . .
Many waters cannot quench love,
neither can floods drown it.

—SONG OF SONGS 8:6-7

Deep love shares in eternity. Whatever is loved lasts forever. Not just the passion of lovers, but spiritual friendship, what the Celts call *anamchara*, as well. Deep love grows souls and gives us resiliency to face life's crises.

Let us give thanks for love that heals and strengthens, even beyond death. May the love we've experienced inspire us to support loving relationships everywhere, so that all the colors of the rainbow might reflect God's beauty.

Spirit, enable me to look beyond imperfection to deeper Love. Let me see Christ disguised in my companions—in the challenges I face with partners, friends, and family members.

66.

My doctor's love for me
is as important as chemotherapy.

—RACHEL NAOMI REMEN

Years ago, physician Bernie Siegel spoke of "love, medicine, and miracles." Medicine cures. Love heals. Those of us who are professionals—whether physicians, nurses, professors, pastors, social workers, or counselors—know that professional expertise alone is not enough to effect healing in those we serve. Love grows our souls and the souls of those entrusted in our

care. As the saying goes, they don't care what you know until they know that you care. Equal parts of medicine and love transform cells and souls.

Let love be your goal and your practice, personally, relationally, and professionally.

Let me join love with expertise and compassion with curing, Spirit, so that those entrusted to my care may grow in spirit as well as body.

67.

God bless the corners of
this house and all the lintel blessed,
And bless the hearth and
bless the board and bless each place of rest,
And bless each door that
opens wide to strangers as to kin,
And bless each crystal window pane
that lets the starlight in,
And bless the rooftree overhead
and every sturdy wall.
The peace of humankind,
the peace of God, with peace and love for all.

—IRISH BLESSING

Home can be healing. Our households can be thin places where heaven and earth meet. Every meal can be eucharistic and every touch healing when dedicated to God.

Let us see hearth and home as holy, viewing our household companions, human and non-human, as messengers of God. Let our households heal everyone who enters. Let giving and receiving be one in the intricate ecology of blessing that shapes our homes and radiates out into the Universe.

Thank You, Spirit, for hearth and home. Give me patience and compassion, love and forgiveness, seeing the holiness of my household companions and bringing forth their holiness in our daily lives together.

68.

I will soothe you and heal you,
I will bring you roses.
I too have been covered with thorns.

—RUMI

Healing relationships are based on spiritual and emotional solidarity. We are all broken and in need of wholeness. Our hearts are wounded and in need of understanding.

We need to see beyond the disguises of impatience, orneriness, anger, and tears, to see the holiness—the original wholeness—of those who have been placed in our lives. We need to see the

angel hidden in the boulders. The light hidden in darkness. The love hidden in struggle. We are called to live by forgiveness—giving and receiving forgiveness on the road to healing so that we might through love bring healing and wholeness to our lives and the lives of our companions.

I thank You, Spirit, for Your presence in the beautiful imperfections of myself and my loved ones. Help me experience our unity, despite difference. Help me find healing in our woundedness. Help me live by love and not fear as we walk the path of healing.

69.

Let everything that breathes praise God.

—PSALM 150:6

We live in a Universe of praise. Even the stars pray, as theologian Jay McDaniel avers. Wherever there is life, there is gratitude and praise. Praise for the Giver of Life. For the Energy of Love that flows through the Universe. For Evolutionary Wisdom, joining purpose, creativity, freedom, and chance. For Existence itself, the wonder of our being and the wonder of all Being.

When we praise God and give thanks, we are in tune with the Universe and reveal holiness in space and time. When we give thanks, our prob-

lems still exist, our struggles are still real, but they become only one aspect of our wonderful world.

Life has changed for us during this year of pandemic and protest. I weep every day for the mounting death toll, and the systemic injustice of our nation saddens and angers me. Yet, in this time, I have found that praise connects me in ways that deepen my commitment to change the world. With the hope grounded in praise, I know I can make a difference, and when I join other voices of praise, the world is transformed.

Thank You, Spirit, for this glorious world. Thank You for the wonder of life and the power of love and beauty flowing in all things. May I not forget that I am healed and strengthened when I praise You.

70.

For all that has been—thanks!
For all that shall be—yes!

—DAG HAMMARSKJOLD

German mystic Meister Eckhardt proclaimed that if the only prayer you make is "thank You," that will be sufficient. Centuries later United Nations Secretary-General Dag Hammarskjold confessed the power of gratitude to transform past, present, and future. Hammarskjold knew tragedy and pain. He saw genocide and war. Yet he also saw Divine Providence moving through his life and all creation. He discovered that in struggle, there is grace. In challenge,

there is hope. He found that by saying "thank You," God and he became partners, opening up the future in its myriad possibilities.

Gratitude not only changes the past; it also transforms our vision of the future. We become part of God's great "yes," the power of the future to inspire us to align ourselves with the moral and spiritual arcs of history. "Yes" is the word that opens the future. We give thanks for new possibilities as we awaken every morning. We rejoice in the opportunity to be God's companions in healing the world one moment at a time.

Thank You, Spirit, for beauty and wonder, for life and love. Let my gratitude inspire a great "yes" as I take my part in healing the Earth.

71.

If our religion is based on salvation,
our chief emotions will be fear and trembling.
If our religion is based on wonder,
our chief emotion will be gratitude.

—CARL JUNG

Rabbi Abraham Joshua Heschel once said, "Never once in my life did I ask God for success or wisdom or power or fame. I asked for wonder, and he gave it to me." Too many people see religion as a transactional process: if I do and believe the "right" things, I will be saved. If I doubt or struggle with faith, or fail at being my

best, I will be punished. In contrast, I agree with Jung and Heschel that authentic spirituality is about wonder and gratitude.

When we see the world as wonder-full, our hearts expand. We reach out to others. We worship God in gratitude and love. Fear-based faiths persecute and exclude. Love-based faiths affirm and include. We choose to honor the wonder of each creature and ourselves and trust that God's work is never finished for us or anyone. God always has more love, adventure, healing, and surprise in store for all of us.

Fill my heart with wonder and love today, Spirit. Let love be my goal and my faith. Let wonder guide my steps.

72.

Do ordinary things with extraordinary love. . . .
Let's do something beautiful for God.

—MOTHER TERESA

M ost days are ordinary for all of us. We wake up, go to the bathroom, eat, interact with others, make decisions, do some form of work, enjoy entertainment, send email, participate in online games or social media, and go to sleep again. Obviously, the specifics of what we do differ, and our global impact may differ. Still, in the routine of life, holiness is found. We can do the ordinary acts of life with great love and devotion.

We can make a phone call with love, send an email with love, cook and clean with love, make executive decisions with love. We can decide to do something beautiful for God in every encounter, choosing to add to the beauty rather than ugliness of the world—and in doing so we help to heal not only the world around us but ourselves as well.

Our lives are our gifts to God. They matter to the quality of God's experience. Let us do something beautiful for God. Let us open up greater possibilities for Divine healing in our lives. Let us give beauty to our Creator and Companion.

`

Artist of the Universe, inspire me to beauty and love. Let my life be a work of art, dedicated to You and my fellow-creatures, bringing joy and beauty to the world.

73.

The world is saved by beauty.

—FYODOR DOSTOEVSKY

Many of us suffer from constricted spirits. Our hearts and senses are closed to the world in its diversity. We are apathetic toward the suffering of others. Our bodies may be healthy, but our spirits are diseased. We need, like Charles Dickens's Scrooge or Dr. Suess's Grinch, to be transformed by wonder and enlightened by beauty. We need to have transformed hearts, minds, and senses to embrace beauty all around us.

Beauty saves because it heals our spirits. It takes us from isolated and insulated self-interest to love for creation. It frees us from fear of life and death. It liberates us from needing enemies and scapegoats to feel good about ourselves. The world is saved by transformed visions that awaken us to the light in ourselves—the light that heals our bodies, minds, and spirits—and the light in all creation that inspires us to love greatly. In loving greatly, we recognize our identity as God's beloved children, gifted with eternity in the midst of daily life and hope for a never-ending journey of adventures with our Creator and all creation.

Transform my heart, Spirit; awaken my senses; energize my arms and legs to walk in love and beauty, large-hearted and loving, freed from fear and death.

74.

The teleology [aim] of the Universe
is toward the production of Beauty.

—ALFRED NORTH WHITEHEAD

I have a running joke with my theological students: I tell them about the Hubble photo of two galaxies, one of which has its spiral arm around the other. I quip, "I wonder if there will be a third galaxy next year!"

We live in a beautiful Universe. Although we can see it through the eyes of mechanistic causation, as mere survival of the fittest, of directionless matter in motion without any purpose or goal, we can also see the Universe striving for

beauty, cooperation, and creativity. Crows can learn (and they are often more patient than my grandchildren!). Trees communicate with one another. Plants appear to reach out to insects. Within what appears to be mechanism and stimulus response is the counterforce of wisdom and complexity, aiming at a world of beauty and wonder. All things possess an inner energy, an inner guidance, inspired by God's constantly evolving creative wisdom. Our choice is to companion with that wisdom to make our world a place of beauty and love, and to bring gladness to all creation.

Creative Wisdom and Love, let me mirror Your creativity, love, and wisdom in my world, creating along with You something holy and beautiful.

75.

When we walk a tree-lined trail
or hike along a mountain stream,
we know that we are on that path
that Meister Eckhart said is
"Beautiful and pleasant and joyful and familiar."

—PATRICIA ADAMS FARMER

We are healed by beauty. The perception of beauty calms and inspires. Patients in hospital rooms with windows that open to the world tend to recover more quickly and experience less pain than those who lack a vision of the horizon. Beauty inspires and thus energizes our cells and souls. With so many people struggling with

stressful lives, leading often to stress-related illnesses, we need horizons of beauty to put our lives in perspective and liberate us from "hurry sickness," the perception that we have too little time and creativity to respond to the challenges of life.

I have discovered that when I walk the beaches of Cape Cod, many of the aches and pains attending my nearly seventy years disappear. I am sure it is partly a matter of blood flow and energizing the body's recuperative processes. It is also a matter of an expanded vision that diminishes the importance of my aches, pains, and anxieties.

Let beauty be your companion each day and you will experience eternity in the flow of time.

Inspire me, Spirit, to seek out beautiful places to feed and heal my spirit.

76.

Today, like every other day,
we wake up empty and frightened.
Don't open the door to the study and begin reading.
Take down the dulcimer.
Let the beauty we love be what we do.
There are a hundred ways
to kneel and kiss the ground.

—RUMI

Beauty takes many forms, revealed in every encounter and moment of our lives. There are a hundred ways—no, hundreds of ways!—to kneel and kiss the ground. In a time of fear and

emptiness, we can look more deeply and see love hidden in fear and beauty hidden in ugliness.

While study is important—Rumi was also a scholar—we need to immerse ourselves in music, dance, touch, and play. We need to integrate senses, heart, mind, and spirit. Do something beautiful, something that does not "toil or spin," or compute. Something that is simply beautiful in this moment with no expectations other than being present in this Holy Here and Now. Rejoice in beauty in this moment, the wonder of your being, and the awesome Creator.

Empower me, Spirit, to join my own and others' pain with the beauty of the Universe. Let me experience the tragic beauty and wonder of life, immersed in this Holy Here and Now.

77.

With beauty before me may I walk.
With beauty behind me may I walk.
With beauty above me may I walk.
With beauty all around me may I walk.

—NAVAJO BLESSING

These days, I walk daily on Cape Cod's beaches. With every breeze and wave, I embrace the beauty of this good Earth. Beauty is everywhere. When I spent a sabbatical year in Washington, DC, I discovered a shady glen just a block from our high rise. Every day my toddler grandson and I rejoiced in the quiet oasis, stream, and trees.

169

The world began in the quest for beauty, and all things are completed in beauty. Wherever we go, we are surrounded by beauty. Wherever we go, God is with us. Wherever we go, we can experience inspiration, joy, and love. With beauty all around us, we walk—and we are made whole.

I rejoice with beauty all around me. I rejoice in the ubiquity of revelation and love that You give me. All places are holy. All places inspired. All places grounded in beauty.

78.

The idea of jazz is like
... people coming together,
listening to one another,
respecting one another's talents,
and trying to create
something beautiful together. ...
As they play together,
they trust in the availability of fresh possibilities.

—JAY MCDANIEL

The many become one and are increased by one. Healing of persons and communities comes through a type of "centered pluralism" in which we hold diversity and unity, difference and oneness, and disagreement and common ground

in creative tension. As we embrace our multiplicity, new creative unities emerge, building on the past and leaning toward the future. Healing also comes from embracing the many aspects of ourselves, not just one perspective or gift. Even God is a creative unity; we call God's centered pluralism the Trinity. The Divine is not a homogenous, static God, but lively, complex, mirrored in our world as "he, she, they," and beyond.

What new aspect of yourself is waiting to emerge? What new gift can bring healing to your life? What unopened parts of yourself await your discovery and creativity?

Artist of the Universe, I give thanks for the multiplicity of life, the contrasts among people and perspectives, and the wonderful multiplicity of my own life.

79.

Look God,
you took great big handfuls of chaos
and made galaxies. . . .
I take paint and crayon and paper
and make worlds, too, along with you.

—MADELEINE L'ENGLE

We are healed by creativity and wonder. Think of the children and grandchildren in your midst. From one day to the next they are superheroes, star athletes, adventurers to other planets. Out of a stick and a few pieces of paper they can create a shield, lightsaber, or house.

Growing up can expand, and not limit, our imaginations. Out of twenty-six letters and a

handful of quotes, I am writing this book, which will end up being over 25,000 words! Gazing at a cloud, I can visualize caravans, warriors, and gods and goddesses in the spirit of First American and Greek mythmakers, whose imaginative myths are much closer to the deepest realities of life than the "realism" of two-dimensional tabulators! When we create, we bring order out of chaos, novelty out of tradition, universes out of raw materials.

What universes are ready to come forth from your creativity? From the materials of your life, what new creation is waiting to be born? What healing will emerge when you allow yourself to create and imagine?

Creative Artist, let my imagination soar, bringing forth new possibilities out of the materials of my life.

80.

Be thou my vision, O Lord of my heart,
Naught be all else to me, save that thou art;
Be thou my best thought in the day and the night,
Both waking and sleeping,
Thy presence my light.

—CELTIC PRAYER

God is the ultimate visionary. God imagines the possibilities of Divine-creature creativity. God births the moral and spiritual arcs of history and embodies them in possibilities right for the moment—and then lets go of the results. God delights when we experience the Divine vision and then embody it in our own unique way. God says,

"Surprise Me. Do something new. Give birth to a new thought, a new way of life, an unexpected adventure."

The goal of life is to embody God's vision in our time and place by our agency, creating something new beyond the vision we have been given. With our children and grandchildren, we are the Harry Potters and Hermiones, the Bilbos and Frodos, the indigenous explorers and scientific adventures, the Dumbledores, Gandalfs, and Minerva McGonagalls. We are everyday people whose daily lives transform the Universe one step at a time, looking toward God's far horizon, and bringing beauty right where we are.

Be my vision, Loving Spirit. Be the vision that guides my daily steps. Be the horizon toward which I journey as Your companion.

81.

There is no greater agony
than bearing the untold story inside of you.

—MAYA ANGELOU

It has been said that God created humanity because God loves stories. There is a story within each of us. There is a novel waiting to be written. A work of art emerging from the puzzle of our lives. A symphony from sharing our stories. Don't stifle your story. Listen to your life and then let it speak in words, melodies, colors, dance, song, caresses, and adventures.

History, we are told, is written by the winners, while losers are forgotten. This is not God's

way. God evokes all our stories and wants us to help others tell theirs. Whose stories are not being heard? Who is forgotten in the histories you read? What voices are silenced and diminished? Whose stories are foreign to you? Be a midwife of others' stories. Let your voice harmonize with voices across the planet, celebrating God's unique and wondrous diversity. Telling our stories and awakening the stories of others is a spiritual and ethical task, one that brings inner and outer healing.

Divine Storyteller, teach me to listen to my life and share it gracefully with others. Help me nurture others' stories: forgotten stories, dismissed stories, oppressed stories, silenced stories.

82.

In the ten years since the tumor was found,
I've published thirteen books.

—REYNOLDS PRICE

When faced with a crisis, we can give up or we can go forward. We can be defeated by the slings and arrows of fate, or we can find creativity hidden in catastrophe. There is a movement toward wholeness in every moment of experience. There is a possibility of healing when there can't be a cure. New horizons can emerge where we see no way forward.

Author Reynolds Price discovered words flowing from the initial terror of spinal cord cancer.

Adventure and creativity, the gifts of spiritual and artistic resilience, are born when out of the rubble of life, we create masterpieces of human experience. The work is not easy, and death, debilitation, despair lurk in the shadows. Trauma surfaces. Injustice cramps. And yet these can be the birth pangs of artistry that changes the world. Ask Maya Angelou, Vincent van Gogh, Helen Keller, Frederick Douglass. Though the machinations of life seek to undermine us, we can become more than we could ever have imagined.

Enable me, Spirit, to rise on eagle's wings of creativity. Empower me to face pain and trauma with courage. Even while I struggle, may I choose the path of adventure, creativity, victory, and love.

83.

Every single one of us, without exception,
is called to co-create with God.
No one is too unimportant
to have a share in the making
or unmaking of the final shining-forth.
Everything that we do
either draws the Kingdom of love closer,
or pushes it further off.

—MADELEINE L'ENGLE

There are many paths to healing and wholeness. For some, it is beauty. For others, ser-

vice. Others discover healing in artistry, whether paints or words. Still, others find wholeness in facing trauma and disease. God is present in every healing path. Every healing path involves sharing in Divine creativity.

Following our calling as co-creators, regardless of our life situation, places our lives in a larger perspective. We are part of the Divine work, and in this alignment, we can experience healing in every season of life, even in facing death, tipping the scales of life from hate to love and ugliness to beauty.

Poet of the Universe, may my life become a work of art, adding to the beauty of Your Universe. Let me contribute to Your work of beauty, justice, goodness, and love.

84.

To age gracefully requires
that we stop denying the fact of aging
and learn and practice what we have to do
to keep our bodies and minds
in good working order
through all the phases of life.

—ANDREW WEIL

Life is a perpetual perishing, the philosopher Alfred North Whitehead said. There is no way to avoid the aging process or our own mortality. But, as holistic physician Andrew Weil asserts, we can practice healthy aging by practicing well-being on a daily basis.

There are many ways to age creatively and gracefully. Movement and diet. Prayer and meditation. Intellectual challenge and empathy. Rest and activity. Self-care and mission. Contemplation and political activism. Being a good ancestor. What we do today transforms our tomorrow. Our values in the present moment shape the contours of the future.

What is your vision of aging? What practices most enhance that vision? Day by day, you can live joyfully and add to the joy you will experience in the decades ahead.

Giver of Life and Health, I thank You for the opportunity to live fully and with wholeness. Help me to follow Your path of healing with each new day, living joyfully in the now and preparing faithfully for the future.

85.

Age puzzles me. I thought it was a quiet time . . .
but my eighties are passionate.
I grow more intense as I age. . . ,
as though I still owed a debt to life.

—FLORIDA SCOTT-MAXWELL

Author Florida Scott-Maxwell, like Dylan Thomas, counsels, that you not go gentle into the night! Change the things you can't accept! Aging is not about rusting out but flaming forth in passion.

We need to not only heal the past and its memories, but be good ancestors whose lives

heal a future we will never live to see. Aging can mean passion not apathy, involvement not isolation, political protest and not passivity. The world needs passionate and prophetic healers. Lively aging and passionate involvement energize us and transform the world. We become healthy ancestors whose passions create a beautiful future for generations to come.

Spirit, inspire passion in my spirit. Energize my cells and soul to be a good ancestor, actively working to bring justice, joy, and peace to the world.

86.

In Hinduism, the one who embarks
on a spiritual quest
after retirement is the sannyasi,
whose example of the final great quest
is legend in society. . . .
In this person is embodied
the best the culture has to offer,
the sign of what is to become
as better people as we age.

—JOAN CHITTISTER

Joan Chittister—Benedictine nun, theologian,
and spiritual guide—invites us to imagine
big spiritual possibilities for ourselves. We are

all little Christs, Bodhisattvas in the making, shamans in preparation, and great Queens and Kings of Narnia ready to enter the wardrobe. Our vision of the future shapes how we live today. In the Holy Here and Now, far horizons call us to create our values in the present moment.

Don't imagine yourself as small-spirited. Think of yourself as a saint, a being of light and love today. The light will lure you forward step by step to become the person God calls you to be, whole and alive, in this moment and in your everlasting journey.

Let me imagine greatness in myself, Spirit. Let me see myself as a Jedi in training, a saint on the way, a Bodhisattva transforming the world, and a little Christ healing creation— and then let this guide each day's values.

87.

The greater the force of your compassion,
the greater your resilience
in confronting hardships.

—DALAI LAMA

Many professionals suffer from what is described as compassion fatigue. It has become epidemic in this time of pandemic when health-care professionals, swamped by patient care and overwhelmed by deaths due to COVID-19, are on the verge of burning out. Their breaking hearts are leaking energy and vitality. They need our thanks. They need our understanding. They need our love. They also need our resources and social responsibility.

Compassion fatigue and burnout are real, and the Dalai Lama is aware of this. He knows that an open heart feels the pain of the world. That is the wisdom of the Bodhisattva and Christ. But an open heart needs to be sustained by relational support, community affirmation, and spiritual practice. Resilience is the result of healthy communities providing spiritual and relational resources for those who bear the stresses of pain and disease.

Let us advocate for a society committed to healing by providing emotional and spiritual support, a willingness to sacrifice for the greater good, and a commitment to embody our gratitude in moving from self-interest to community and planetary loyalty.

Loving Spirit, let me support those who support others.

88.

I'm not sure if resilience is ever achieved alone.
. . . If we have someone who loves us—
I don't mean who indulges us,
but who loves us enough to be on our side—
then it's easier to grow resilience,
to grow belief in self,
to grow self-esteem. And it's self-esteem
that allows a person to stand up.

—MAYA ANGELOU

It takes a village to raise a child—and it takes a community to support our spiritual growth. Widespread resilience emerges from communities of com-

passion, caring, and challenge. Children need adults who believe in them, see their gifts, and challenge them to moral, spiritual, practical, relational, and intellectual excellence. Adults need others to show them the path to understanding and achievement.

Healing and wholeness are active and proactive, not just reactive. Our task is to heal persons' lives in advance. To inoculate persons against low self-esteem and low expectations early in life so that they live joyful and healthy adult lives. The support of others allows us to relax, grow in wisdom, and find resources to make a way where we saw a dead end.

Loving Spirit, inspire us to create healthy communities, supportive of self-esteem and excellence.

89.

It demands great spiritual resilience
not to hate the hater whose foot is on your neck,
and an even greater miracle
of perception and charity
not to teach your child to hate.

—JAMES BALDWIN

As I write these words, we are in a time of political division. When I look at my news feed, I feel angry and want to lash out, wanting to cut down to size Facebook friends who align themselves with those whom I believe are destroying our nation. Then, I pause and remember that hate and irrational anger will not bring peace to the world. Anger

without understanding and forgiveness will only add to the divisiveness and violence. I train my vision to see something of God in the oppressor. The fomenters of hate, whether in white nationalist groups or national leaders encouraging division, are harming their own souls. Their hate is destroying them, and it can destroy me if I succumb to hatred. I must fight for justice and democracy but do so with love and reconciliation in my heart.

This is the source of prophetic healing. Changing our world as we change ourselves. Courageously facing down evil without becoming evil ourselves.

God of all peoples, give me courage to be a prophet and a healer, saving my soul as I work to heal the souls of oppressed and oppressor.

90.

Spiritual resilience is not
simply about recovering from adversity.
It is about bouncing back
in a way that deeper knowledge
of both God and self may result . . .
to nurture our relationship with God
and enable it to grow in surprising ways.

—ROBERT WICKS

Difficult times can destroy us. They can also
deepen our spirits, according to psychologist
and spiritual guide Robert Wicks. God is present
in moments of dark and light, and in agitation
and comfort, to inspire healing, wholeness, and

spiritual growth. God does not place sickness and tragedy in our lives, and God is not the source of cancer, accidental injury, or violence—but God is within those moments of despair.

Even when we find ourselves in the depths, God's light still shines. Even when we have done something that we believe is unforgivable, God is ready to welcome us home, show us a new path, and give us the courage to make amends. As the apostle Paul affirms, "Nothing can separate us from the love of God" (Romans 8:38). Times of stress and brokenness can become moments of healing and growth when we place them in God's care and listen for God's guidance.

Loving Companion, You are the Fellow Sufferer who understands. Help me trust You in darkness as well as light.

91.

When we are no longer able to change a situation,
we are challenged to change ourselves. . . .
Everything can be taken
from a man but one thing:
the last of the human freedoms—
to choose one's attitude
in any given set of circumstances,
to choose one's own way.

—VIKTOR FRANKL

Psychiatrist and Holocaust survivor Viktor
Frankl knew the power of taking responsibility for our lives even in the most difficult situ-

ations. We cannot fully determine our environment, the political context, our health condition, or the success of our projects. Our freedom to choose and agency may be limited by the decisions of others and the accidents of life. Still, we are not without spiritual resources. Our response to what we cannot control may be a matter of life and death, spiritually, emotionally, or physically for us and others.

We are free to choose how we respond to adversity and loss. We are free to choose life, love, agency, and health, even in the midst of death, hatred, helplessness, and sickness.

Show me, loving Spirit, where my freedom lies, and let me use my freedom to choose love for myself and those around me.

92.

It did not really matter what we expected from life,
but rather what life expected from us.
We needed to stop asking about the meaning of life,
and instead to think of ourselves as those
who were being questioned by life—
daily and hourly.
Our answer must consist,
not in talk and meditation,
but in right action and in right conduct.

—VIKTOR FRANKL

The events of life challenge us to be creative, open-hearted, loving, and compassionate. Each day presents decisions and surprises by

which we shape our character and those around us. Healing and wholeness come from moment-by-moment decisions, often appearing to be inconsequential, but over a lifetime molding our characters and impact on the world. We have a place in the Universe no one else can fill, influencing in large or small ways those touched by our lives momentarily or over a lifetime. Each moment is a holy adventure, calling us to choose love and healing, to bring light to the world, and say "yes" to the wonder of the Universe.

With each new day, Spirit, help me to choose love and life, to send ripples of healing across the Universe, beginning with my own integrity and agency, and expanding to family, friends, my community, and the planet. Let me be a light-bearer and love-giver.

93.

The curious paradox is that when I accept myself just as I am, then I can change.

—CARL ROGERS

Many of us are more judgmental in terms of ourselves than we are toward others. We condemn our mistakes. We see ourselves as stupid, ugly, unworthy. But self-condemnation harms rather than heals. It denies our full humanity and makes it impossible to embrace and heal those parts of ourselves we hate or deny.

Self-acceptance is not passivity. Nor does it condone bad behavior on our part. It has been

said that one of Jesus' unique gifts was that he accepted people just as they were but did not leave them there. His love inspired change. His acceptance inspired transformation, just as recognizing both our wonder and imperfection, our stature and small-mindedness, plants seeds of growth. We cannot heal what we choose not to know or deny. Acceptance opens us to self-awareness and self-discovery, and sets us on the path of whole-person healing.

Help me accept myself just as I am, Spirit, and in embracing my whole self, give me the courage to change and grow into Your vision for my unique life.

94.

Be grateful for your life, every detail of it,
and your face will come to shine like a sun,
and everyone who sees it
will be made glad and peaceful.

—RUMI

In gratitude, I embrace the past, using both fail-
ure and success as the materials out of which
I create a life of beauty, service, and compassion
today. Though it was painful, and I wish much
of it had not occurred, I am grateful for our family's struggles with mental-health issues and

unemployment. We were survivors! I learned how to minister to people with emotional challenges and be compassionate toward persons experiencing economic hardship and food insecurity. I wouldn't want to repeat the painful past, but I also wouldn't want to nullify it. I am what I am today due to my choices to accept past pain, grow from it, and allow it to open my heart. God is at work in every circumstance of life. In giving thanks, I intuit God's presence and make my wounds an instrument for the healing of others.

Thank You, Spirit, for awakening me this morning. Thank You for life itself and my unique life. Let me use my life experiences in the healing of myself and the world.

95.

In all my experience
as a psychiatrist and as a human being,
the deepest, most pervasive pathology I have seen
is the incredible harshness
we have toward ourselves. . . .
Simply bring a little kindness
toward yourself from time to time. . . .
It is in this atmosphere
that your basic sanity can grow.

—GERALD MAY

Jesus affirmed the healing power of self-love.
He was always showing his followers that they
were more than they imagined, that they could

move life's mountains with faith as small as a mustard seed. Jesus told simple fishermen, outcasts, and persons with mental illness and disabilities that they were the salt of the earth and the light of the world.

We need to be gentle toward ourselves, as psychiatrist and spiritual guide Gerald May counsels, seeking to understand ourselves, accept responsibility for our moral failings, and move forward toward possibilities hidden within imperfection. Healing is concealed in our pain, giftedness in our limitations, understanding in our ethical failures, and patience in our spiritual struggles. Self-love ultimately finds completion in loving others.

Spirit, let me be kind to myself, and may that become a catalyst for kindness that liberates the self-affirmation and giftedness of others.

96.

We cannot change the past,
but we can change our attitude toward it.
Uproot guilt and plant forgiveness.
Tear out arrogance and seed humility.
Exchange love for hate—
thereby making the present comfortable
and the future promising.

—MAYA ANGELOU

Poet Maya Angelou had a history of trauma and challenge, as well as her own share of failures. Yet she knew that the past can be a foundation for growth and transformation, creativity

and compassion. Guilt only constricts the spirit. Hate destroys our souls. Forgiveness and love awaken us to an abundant Universe in which even the limitations and pain of the past become the impetus for creativity and adventure.

The past is real—it happened. It can't be undone. But the past can be healed, even transformed. We can become new persons. God's mercies are new every morning.

Let the joys and sorrows of the past, Spirit, be catalysts to creative and compassionate transformation.

97.

First, we are challenged
to rise above the narrow confines
of our individualistic concerns
to the broader concerns of all humanity.
. . . We are links in the great chain of humanity. . . .
We have before us the glorious opportunity
to inject a new dimension of love
into the veins of our civilization.

—MARTIN LUTHER KING JR.

Healthy life involves the movement from self-interest to care for our community and nation and to an even wider circle of world loyalty. Planetary healing depends on us going beyond nation

first, recognizing that we are not only in the same boat, but, as one pandemic commentator noted, we are all in the same storm.

Generosity is an antidote to the defensiveness and anxiety of self-interest and nationalism. The small self and the isolated nation are always under threat. Enemies are everywhere. Another's gain is our loss. Another's success threatens our well-being. Large souls and large-souled nations live by abundance. They work to bring health and healing to the planet, even if it means sacrificing economic largesse. The greater good involves life, liberty, and the pursuit of happiness not only for all human-kind, but for all beings. Let us live abundantly and lovingly, seeing all life as holy and interdependent.

Let me seek the well-being of all creatures, Spirit.

98.

I should like a lake of finest ale
for the king of kings.
I should like a table of the choicest food
for the family of heaven.
Let the ale be made from the fruits of the earth
and the food be forgiving love.
I should welcome the poor to my feast,
for they are God's children.
I should welcome the sick to my feast,
for they are God's joy.

—BRIGID OF KILDARE

The Celtic saint Brigid proclaimed the unity of justice and celebration. The heart of spiritual

healing—not to mention political healing—is found in sharing the bounties of life. Spiritual healing is about laughter, reconciliation, friendship, playfulness. Justice is about liberating the imagination of children, awakening children to dreams, and then helping them achieve them. Justice means families have enough food, happy homes, safe neighborhoods and schools, healthy environments, and peace and joy in city streets and country roads. God's healing realm is a feast in which everyone is invited and all creation rejoices. Our healing depends on the healing of our nation, our community, and the planet. Our healing heals our community, nation, and planet.

Holy One, inspire me to generosity and compassion. Let my largesse be a gift to others and my success bring joy to all creation.

99.

Praised be You, my Lord,
through our Sister Bodily Death,
from whom no living man can escape.

—FRANCIS OF ASSISI

During the days of pandemic, I was reminded of my mortality. When I donned my mask for my sunrise walk, I recognized the reality that I was at risk, based on age and health condition. When I kept safe distancing and canceled in-person worship due to a rise of COVID-19 cases on Cape Cod, I was aware of the mortality of the congregants whom I have come to love. I am not afraid of death—but I know it is real and ulti-

mately cannot be avoided. Can I learn to praise God at the descending edges of life?

Filled with a sense of God's nearness, Francis penned the words of his prayer when he was on his deathbed. He knew that death was not the end. He even burst out in poetry and song as he anticipated God's ultimate healing touch. The ultimate healing is experiencing peace with death on the horizon. Death ends this lifetime, and we can grieve the loss of friends and family and this good Earth, but death also awakens us to God's everlasting life, where sunrise and sunset are one and all creation rejoices. The One who loved us into life receives us with loving arms at death. Thanks be to God!

Let me trust my living and dying to You, O Spirit, living fully and at peace regardless of what happens in life and death. Let me know that nothing can separate me from Your love.

100.

Even though I walk through the darkest valley,
I fear no evil; for you are with me;
your rod and your staff—they comfort me. . . .
Surely goodness and mercy shall follow me
all the days of my life, and I shall dwell
in the house of the LORD my whole life long.

—PSALM 23:4,6

Virtually all the Jewish and Christian scrip-
tures were written in times of threat. Enemy
forces outside the city gates. Coups and uprisings
on the horizon. Persecution and imprisonment.

Sickness and death. Regret over past misdeeds. And God was there, present in the darkness.

God creates a circle of light even in the night. An abundant meal with enemies outside our tent. God will bless us and keep us despite the threats of life. We will dwell in the house of God not only our whole life long but forever. There is something more than mortality. Even in the midst of death is the everlasting love of the God who heals the sick, comforts the fearful, and gives new life to the dying. In God's eternal presence, we have a never-ending place to heal, grow, and praise forever.

Bless my living and dying, Spirit. Let me know that You are with me in light and dark, and health and illness—and You will receive me with loving arms at the end of my journey.

101.

May the road rise up to meet you.
May the wind be always at your back.
May the sun shine warm upon your face;
the rains fall soft upon your fields
and until we meet again, may God hold you
in the palm of His hand.

—CELTIC BLESSING

We conclude this adventure in healing and wholeness with awareness of the blessedness of life. We are blessed to be a blessing. Our blessing is part of a deeper blessing, God's all-encompassing love. No matter the challenges that

surround us, we are in the palm of God's hand, and God still has work for us to do to bring God's realm to earth as it is in heaven. Encompassed by love, we experience the ultimate and everlasting healing: God above us, God below us, God in front of us, God behind us—God coming to us in every moment and every event. Blessed at home and on the road, in living and dying, always in the palm of God's hand.

May I experience Your blessing in every encounter, Spirit. May I feel blessed in times of sorrow and joy. May I feel peace in calm, as well as conflict. May I be blessed as I protest and as I pray. May I find healing and wholeness in Your endless blessing that is the beginning and end of all things.

Acknowledgment

I am grateful to Ellyn Sanna for asking me to participate in the Soul Seeds series of which this book is my third contribution. Ellyn seeks to bring forth the values of healing and wholeness as publisher of Anamchara Books. I am also grateful to Valerie Zehl for her affirmative editorial support.

101 Soul Seeds

for Grandparents Working for a Better World

Grandparenting is truly a holy adventure. As we see and bring forth the inner divinity of our grandchildren, we have the opportunity to show them that they are not only our beloved grandchildren but God's children as well, infinite in worth and possibility.

This book is an invitation to consider grandparenting as a spiritual and ethical vocation. As we commit ourselves to love and pray for our grandchildren, we can also work to create a just and healthy world for all grandchildren.

Paperback Price: $12.99

Kindle Price: $4.99

101 Soul Seeds

Peacemakers & Justice-Seekers

Authentic spirituality embeds us in the pain of the world and inspires commitment to social justice and conflict resolution. This book is intended to support your integration of peacemaking, justice-seeking, and spiritual growth. You have a calling to be God's companion in healing the world—one relationship, phone call, and protest at a time. The journey may be long and difficult, but the path of contemplative activism found in this book will restore your spirit, giving you strength and inspiration as you join in God's work of peace and justice.

Paperback Price: $12.99

Kindle Price: $4.99

101 Soul Seeds

for Parents of Adult Children

Being a parent held joys and challenges every step of the way, and never more so than when our children finally made it to adulthood. Now we can connect with them on deeper levels than ever—but unexpected potential pitfalls dot this new path we're traveling. *101 Soul Seeds for Parents of Adult Children* offers observations and quotes, coupled with simple prayers to help us navigate this portion of parenting . . . so we and our adult children grow closer to one another and closer to our own souls' destination.

Paperback Price: $12.99

Kindle Price: $4.99

Anamchara
Books

www.AnamcharaBooks.com

Made in the USA
Middletown, DE
13 December 2023